Passion of Christ,
Passion of the World

LEONARDO BOFF

Passion of Christ,
Passion of the World

The Facts, Their Interpretation, and Their Meaning Yesterday and Today

Translated from the Portuguese by
Robert R. Barr

ORBIS BOOKS

Maryknoll, New York 10545

The Catholic Foreign Mission Society of America (Maryknoll) recruits and trains people for overseas missionary service. Through Orbis Books Maryknoll aims to foster the international dialogue that is essential to mission. The books published, however, reflect the opinions of their authors and are not meant to represent the official position of the society.

Originally published as *Paixão de Cristo—Paixão do Mundo,* copyright © 1977 by Editora Vozes Ltda., Rua Frei Luís, 100, 25.600 Petrópolis, Rio de Janeiro

Copyright © 1987 by Orbis Books
Published by Orbis Books, Maryknoll, NY 10545
All rights reserved
Manufactured in the United States of America

All Bible quotations are from *The New American Bible*

Manuscript Editor: William E. Jerman

Library of Congress Cataloging-in-Publication Data
Boff, Leonardo.
  Passion of Christ, passion of the world.

  Translation of: Paixão de Cristo—paixão do mundo.
  Bibliography: p.
  1. Jesus Christ—Crucifixion. 2. Passion narratives
(Gospels)—Criticism, interpretation, etc. 3. Atonement.
I. Title.
BT453.B6313 1987   232.9′6   87-7815
ISBN 0-88344-564-6
ISBN 0-88344-563-8 (pbk.)

To Alceu Amoroso Lima,
friend and teacher,
for his prophetic witness

No authority can decree that everything is permitted; for justice and exploitation are not so indistinguishable. And Christ died so that we might know that not everything is permitted.

José Porfirio Miranda,
Being and the Messiah, p. ix

Contents

Preface

Admittedly, this book is a good deal more experimental in nature than others concerned with the christological mystery. What I am attempting here is an exploration of the meaning of the cross of our Lord Jesus Christ for the context of our contemporary faith and circumstances. It is of the greatest importance to be aware of the locus from which a given discourse is articulated, if we hope to be able to appraise and appreciate its conclusions. In the present case, that locus is the situation of captivity and resistance in which so many human beings live today—a locus very near that from which Jesus of Nazareth looked out upon his own historical reality.

The cross, in a very special way, attracts our attention to Jesus' humanity— which is none other than the humanity of God. One can take a number of different theological positions vis-à-vis the humanity of Jesus Christ. Tradition has crystalized in two of them, and neither has ever lost its currency or its validity. Both are based on the Gospels, as well as on christological dogma as defined at the Council of Chalcedon in the year 451. Chalcedon, infallibly and irreformably, defined for Christian faith of all time to come the true humanity and true divinity of Jesus Christ. In Jesus Christ, in the oneness of the single divine person of the eternal Word, subsist two distinct natures, the divine and the human, without confusion, without change, without division, without separation.

It is this formulation, drawn up at Chalcedon, and so charged with dialectical tension, that renders possible the two lines of christological thinking that have dominated the history of Christian theology ever since. The one approach will emphasize, in Jesus who is at once God and a human being, his divinity. The other will emphasize his humanity. This duality of accent corresponds to two basically different options, giving rise to two distinct schools of christology. In the New Testament, Saint John's Gospel underscores Jesus' divinity, whereas the synoptics stress his humanity. In the ancient world, the school of Alexandria represents the first tendency; Antioch stresses the second. Both schools can fall into heresy. The Alexandrian school will play host to monophysitism, which posits only one nature in Jesus: the divine nature. The Antiochene school will be vulnerable to Arianism, which maintains the distinction of natures in Jesus in such wise as to violate the oneness of his person, and the human nature will dominate in Jesus, with his divinity extrinsic and parallel. In the medieval world the Thomistic school opted to reflect on Jesus from a point of departure in his divinity; the Franciscan school, from his humanity. In modern times we hear of a "descending" christology, or christology "from above," that of a God who becomes incarnate, and an "ascending" christology, one "from below," in which a human Jesus gradually reveals his divinity.

For my own part, on the strength of my spiritual formation and basic option alike, I follow the Franciscan school—the synoptic, Antiochene, and Scotist tradition. I find God precisely in Jesus' total, complete humanity. And a reflection on Jesus' death on the cross affords me an opportunity to rethink his humanity in a radical way.

Accustomed as they are to the traditional image of Jesus, so strongly marked by his divinity, Christians may have difficulty with the image I sketch here—in terms of our own so familiar humanity. And yet we want to open ourselves to the true humanity of Jesus. To the extent that we accept our own humanity, with all the tragedy that may characterize our existence, we open the way for a deep acceptance of the humanity of Jesus. And the converse is equally true: to the extent that we accept Jesus as the Gospels, especially the synoptic Gospels, depict him, living a life charged with conflict and pain—to the extent that we take the incarnation absolutely seriously, as an "emptying," as the total evacuation of divinity—to this same extent we shall accept ourselves, with all our fragility and misery, without shame or humiliation.

My basic option implies consequences of an exegetical and dogmatic order. This option will have an influence on my conception of Jesus' messianic consciousness, how he faced his own death, and how he gradually assimilated, amid trials and temptations, the will of God.

It is my expectation that this theological route will lead to an inestimably precious treasure: the discovery of how we can take up direct discipleship and following of Jesus of Nazareth, who, before us, walked our own human path, and walked it to the very end.

I have no wish to conceal the dangers that will beset someone undertaking this study. I shall try to avoid the pitfalls, in all honesty, keeping rigidly within the bounds of christological dogma set by our Chalcedonian fathers before us. The humanity of which I shall be speaking in this experiment must always be conceived and understood as the humanity of God. To be sure, this will oblige us to question our basic image of God—for today. Our common image of God owes much to pagan and Old Testament religious experience. A reflection on the humanity of Jesus (which is the humanity of God) reveals to us the specifically Christian, unmistakable and unique, face of God. Clearly, then, pagans and Christians experience the same mystery—but in Jesus Christ the face of God is revealed, a surprising face, the face of a lowly sufferer, tortured, smeared with blood, crowned with thorns, and dying after a mysterious, piercing cry hurled at the heavens (but not against heaven). Such a God is extremely close to the human drama, but a strange God, too, marked by a fascinating strangeness, like that of our own innermost depths. Before this God we can stiffen with fear, as did Luther; but we can also be touched with an infinite tenderness, like Saint Francis, who meditated the passion as "compassion." I make no pretense of revealing the source of the light that illumines the spirit of a Francis. My own reflections will seek only to articulate that spirit itself.

I hope that my experiment will be a help to those who, in their pain, seek to confer a meaning on the painful passion of this world. And—who knows?—meditation on the passion of the suffering prophet, Jesus Christ, may awaken in us some unsuspected source of strength for resistance and resurrection. Dramatic times bring with them visions of redemption, and the suffering Christian discovers a secret identification with the prototypical Christian martyr. Then hidden forces burst forth, to transform the warp and woof of the tale of life from within that life itself, to tear away the mask from the face of oppression and look upon its fragile face—fragile because textured by death. History tells us that it is here that life triumphs, and begets a meaning stronger than anything the empire of death can achieve.

This book substantially reflects a course given at the Catholic University of Lisbon in the latter part of 1976. Chapter 2 first appeared in part in *Teología y mundo contemporáneo* (Madrid, 1975), a festschrift for Karl Rahner on his seventieth birthday, and again as a chapter of my *Teologia do cativeiro e da libertação* (Lisbon, 1976). Chapter 7 first appeared in the periodical *Grande Sinal,* 28 (1974) 509-27, and then as a chapter in my *Teologia do cativeiro.* Chapter 9 was first published in the international review *Concilium* (Lisbon), 9 (1976) 6-17.

Chapter 1

Problem and Formulations

GUIDING INTEREST OF THIS INVESTIGATION

Every composition, every piece of research, however objective it may intend to be, is under the commanding influence of a "horizon of interest." To know is to interpret, and there are no exceptions. The hermeneutic structure of all knowledge, all science, is such that the subject of that knowledge or science, with its models, paradigms, and categories, enters into the composition of the experience of the object via the mediation of a language. The subject is not pure reason. The subject is immersed in history, in a socio-political context, and is moved by personal and collective interests. There is no knowing, then, no knowledge, that is free of ideology, that is purely disinterested.

The gospel accounts, particularly those concerning the passion and death of Jesus, are charged with interpretation, inescapably guided by a theological interest. This observation does not imply any depreciation of the Christian message. Like any other historical text, the accounts of the passion are situated within a general hermeneutic structure, and it is within this general hermeneutic structure that they must be interpreted.

What I propose to do is to explicitate a universal procedure that is rarely made explicit in written texts. I shall state my interest in my reading, interpreting, and meditating on the violent death of Jesus Christ. My interest is situated on the horizon of the theology of liberation, of captivity and resistance.

In this "way of doing theology," the theologian elaborates on a threefold experience:

1. The experience of *political, economic, and cultural oppression* of one group by another group. There exists a situation of aggression. It exists at the world level, and it entails grave consequences for entire nations. It consists of hunger, misery, institutionalized international crime, enormously destructive wars, a division between wealthy countries and poor countries—in a word, it amounts to a situation of world injustice.

2. The experience of *liberation movements,* which seek to shake off all yokes and go in search of a new manner of life in common, seek to gestate a

1

new type of human being, one who will be more of a comrade, more open to communion.

3. The experience of *resistance* on the part of dominated but undefeated groups working in a regime of captivity and refusing to let the spark of hope flicker and die.

These three experiences go hand in hand with another, just as profound: that of the unqualified resistance of opulent societies to any structural change, along with their capacity for repressive violence—the ruthless, systematic extermination of all who oppose them. At the same time there is the experience of revolutionary violence, which is capable of crushing everything in its path, eradicating whole populations, and employing violence to impose its new models. Genuine liberation projects, begun in a profound spirit of humaneness and humanity, are expunged by fire and sword. Many Christians, especially in the Third World, have suffered imprisonment and torture, have been sacrificed to the fury of repressive forces, abandoned by their very brothers and sisters in the faith, and left to die of their wounds.

This situation, so common today in the many countries where a "national security" regime is in control, becomes a lens for the reading and interpretation of the passion and death of Jesus Christ. Not a few Christians, undergoing a similar experience of passion and the cross, have felt at one with the suffering servant, have identified with the "man of sorrows," Jesus Christ.

My interest, then, is directed to the detection of the mechanisms that led Jesus to rejection, imprisonment, torture, and a shameful crucifixion. My interest is to demonstrate that this dénouement was a result of a commitment and a praxis that threatened the status quo of his time. I propose to consider how Christ waged this conflict, what meaning he attributed to it, and how it has been interpreted in the New Testament and in the history of reflection guided by faith. Finally, I seek to detail the meaning that the passion and death of Jesus possesses for our faith today as lived and tested in the context of our interest.

This way of posing the question seems to me to be a crucial one. Few subjects in theology have been so manipulated and distorted in their interpretation as that of the cross and death of Jesus Christ. The wealthy sectors of society in particular—the powers that be—have utilized the symbol of the cross and the fact of the redemptive death of Christ to demonstrate the need for suffering and death as part and parcel of human life. Piously and with resignation, it is said, we must all carry our crosses, day by day: the important thing is to carry them with patience and submission; indeed, it is by the cross that we reach the light, and repair the offense done to the infinite majesty of God by our own sins and those of the world.

This manner of discourse is extremely ambiguous, and open to facile manipulation. It ignores the historical death of Jesus, which was a matter neither of blind fate nor of resigned acceptance. It was provoked: its causes lay outside it. And it was executed with violence. It resulted from a praxis on Jesus' part that struck out at the basic elements of society and of the Judaic religion. These latter failed to assimilate Jesus, and finally rejected and repelled him by physical liquidation. This was the price Jesus had to pay for the freedom he had exercised. This was the outcome of the battle he had waged against pharisaism, the privilege of status, legalism, and the hardening of hearts toward God and neighbor. Jesus suffered and died in a struggle with the objective causes of suffering and death, then and now.

An appeal to death and the cross can mask over the injustice of the practices of precisely those who are the ones who manufacture the cross and death of others. This exhortation is nothing more than a vulgar ideology, which—thanks to suffering and death—is free to pursue its subjugation and exploitation, unjust relationships among persons and classes, privileges, and domination. But the cross of Christ cannot be allowed to be interpreted in such a way as to leave the door open for its misuse in this fashion. The glory of God does not consist in human suffering, deprivation, spoliation, and daily crucifixion. The glory of God consists in human life and human happiness. Our God does not have the face of the pagan gods, who envy the happiness of men and women. Our God is a God who impels us toward a manner of living such that the repetition of the drama of the crucifixion of Christ and of other human beings down through history may gradually recede in time. The death of Christ was a crime, not a requirement of the will of a God eager for the reparation of outraged honor, concerned for the esthetics of the divine relationship with humanity. As a Mexican theologian has so well said: "Christ died that we might know that not everything is permitted" (Miranda, *Being and the Messiah,* p. ix). Christ's death means the condemnation of oppressive practices, a denunciation of the mechanisms that spew out suffering and death. It may never be allowed to serve their consecration and legitimation. The cross is never a masochistic symbol. Rather it calls us to a struggle *against* pain, and *against* the causes that produce a cross. Piety and theology alike require the recovery of the historical concreteness of the cross of Jesus Christ, in opposition to its transformation into a pure symbol of resignation and expiation, in line with the mystifications to which any symbol is vulnerable.

Christian hope looks not to the cross, but to the crucified, for he is now the one who lives, the one who was raised up. He is the living and exalted one because God has shown that to be crucified because of identification with the oppressed and the poor of this world has an ultimate sense so bound up with life that it cannot be swallowed up in death. The resurrection preserves its true Christian and eschatological meaning only in intimate connection with the crucifixion. The resurrection is the final sense of insurrection for right and justice. Divorced from this perspective, the resurrection is in danger of mystification—to which the cross has already fallen prey—only this time as the symbol of a world totally reconciled to God for all future time without having to pass by way of a conversion from the causative mechanisms of the wickedness of the present. As we shall see in the course of this study, Christian existence preserves its Christian identity only to the extent that it lives and maintains itself in the paschal dialectic of crucifixion and resurrection as an exigency of the discipleship and following of Jesus Christ. Only then does the gift of meaning yielded by the painful route followed by Jesus Christ leap to our eyes in all its resplendent clarity—and this imposed, enforced death can be accepted as a form of that love of self-oblation that now is bestowed once more on human beings, on all human beings, even executioners. Death, then, is not fatality, but the fruit of liberty. Hans Küng puts it admirably:

> Man has to decide. He can reject this—hidden—meaning; in spite, cynicism, or despair. He can also accept it: in believing trust in him who endowed the senseless suffering and death of Jesus with meaning. Protest, rebellion, or frustration then become superfluous. Despair is at an end [Küng, 433-34].

Before we consider the "trajectory" of Jesus' death, let me place the guiding interest of the gospel accounts of the passion in confrontation with the interest motivating my own theological reading.

GUIDING INTEREST OF THE GOSPEL ACCOUNTS
OF JESUS' PASSION

With reference to the passion and death of Christ in the Gospels, we must consider the following:

1. The texts as we have them were written considerably after the paschal event, and in the light of the major fact of the resurrection. For the New Testament, as for ourselves, the resurrection signifies a whole new dimension of the message and figure of Jesus Christ. It becomes the lens through which that entire message and figure is now reshaped. It becomes the point of departure for christology. In light of the resurrection, the primitive Christian community entered upon the process of interpreting the whole life of Christ. Now all the ambiguity that had hovered over the figure of Jesus was removed. Now it was clear that he was not a false prophet. God had been with him. The God who had seemed to abandon him on Good Friday now appeared as his legitimator. When the communities testify to Jesus, then, and write about him in the Gospels, it is always to the one who was raised up that they bear their witness. In the deeds, the words, the insinuations of the historical Jesus, they now see revelations of the one who was raised up, now interpreted as Son of Man, Son of God, the messiah, and so on.

The Gospels are a testimonial. In them the profession of faith is always present. The evangelists wrote nothing for the sheer pleasure of writing, the enjoyment of recounting something for posterity. Their interest resides in convincing, proclaiming, defending, polemicizing, and testifying to Jesus as the Christ, the savior of humankind. Thus we find in the Gospels, in a unity difficult to sunder, history and theology, account and profession of faith, narrative and dogmatic thesis.

In light of the resurrection, the scandal that was the crucifixion has become intelligible for the disciples. Now they have understood the plan of God. Jesus' death is seen as a moment in that plan. Jesus' death is seen as a passage to resurrection. In the Gospels that death is completely subsumed in the perspective of the good end of the prophet who now has been raised from the dead.

It constituted an immense labor on the part of the primitive church to reconcile the God who abandoned Jesus on the cross with the God who raised him from the dead. The task was always motivated by the same compelling thrust—to bridge the gap separating the two data, to show the oneness of the God acting in each event, together with the oneness of the subject, Jesus Christ, who died and was raised up. Theology, as we shall see in more detail, furnished the categories that made this transition possible.

2. Side by side with this general perspective, that of the resurrection, there is also an apologetic, internal moment. First the phenomenon of Jesus Christ must be rendered intelligible to Jewish converts. Their faith must be strengthened. Hence the importance of citations from the Old Testament—to demonstrate the unity of God's plan, to show the fulfillment of prophecies. For the gospel accounts, the one who suffers, is tortured, and dies is not simply the Jew, Jesus of Nazareth. He is the messiah, the Son of Man, the Son of God. All this is presented in the gospel accounts without explicit polemics, but with a polemical tenor underlying the theological enterprise.

We are familiar with the first polemics to this effect from the Acts of the Apostles. Saint Stephen furiously incriminates the unconverted Jews: "You stiff-necked people, uncircumcised in heart and ears, you . . . have become [the Just One's] betrayers and murderers" (Acts 7:51–52). Peter refers to the crucified one in polemical tones as God's "Servant Jesus, whom you handed over and disowned in Pilate's presence" (Acts 3:13), refers to him as "Jesus Christ the Nazorean whom you crucified" (Acts 4:10), as the one "you put to death, hanging him on a tree" (Acts 5:30). These texts betray the primitive church's latent polemics—polemics not explicit in the passion accounts, but nonetheless present in the explicit assertion that this Jesus, rejected and condemned but now alive again, is the messiah.

3. What is the literary genre of the passion accounts? This question is important, for the literary genre determines the facts and events to be recounted, underscores certain aspects of these facts and events, and conceals dimensions that could lie open to a different understanding of these facts and events. The exegetical literature on this point is enormous in its extent.

We are not dealing with the martyrdom genre, as in the Acts of the Martyrs, although certain elements of it are present. Nor is this the genre of edification; its characteristics are altogether absent. Nor do we have anamnesis, or memorial, here; once again there are some elements present, but not to the point of characterizing the account.

The literary genre of the passion narratives is precisely that of *account*. The passion is being *told, recounted*—not in the modern sense of relating an event, not in terms of the criteria of modern historiography—but nonetheless with the guiding interest of recounting. Recounting what? Recounting the suffering and passion of Jesus, who was the messiah. This is where the dogmatic interest resides. Jesus is the messiah. And the messiah is a suffering messiah. A statement like this was a genuine scandal for a Jewish audience. A messiah who suffers and dies! But this is the statement the Gospels make, and they make it massively. The cross is presented as the identifying symbol of the true messiah. The representations of Judaism concerning the messiah are destroyed. The accounts place the whole blame on the Jews, who have condemned Jesus for no other cause than this basic one that he had been the messiah and had been rejected. The Gospels extract the conclusion of the polemics between Jews and Christians and divest it of its polemical tone: the Jews have killed Christ, liquidated the messiah. The gospel accounts are calculated to fortify the faith of converts and express the self-understanding of the primitive community.

The Gospels also build a bridge, with a view to facilitating the acceptance of the thesis that the messiah suffers because he is the just man, and a suffering just man. As we shall see, Jewish tradition had reflected a great deal on the subject of the suffering just one. Christ is interpreted in the Gospels as the suffering just one, and the messiah.

4. The *Sitz im Leben,* or "situation in life," of the accounts is liturgical. It is geared toward worship. Christians in their gatherings recalled and meditated on the great moments of the Lord's life, death, and resurrection. Thus, in a context of prayer, Acts makes explicit reference to the passion (Acts 4:24–31): after the deliverance of the Apostles, the Christians raise their voices to God, reciting Psalm 2, which the text applies to the passion, adding: "Indeed, they gathered in this very city against your holy Servant, Jesus, whom you anointed—Herod and Pontius Pilate in league with the Gentiles and the peoples of Israel" (Acts 4:27).

The principal object of proclamation and celebration in the liturgy is the salvific activity of God. Human beings come on the scene as actors in a drama directed from on high. No longer is blame assigned, no longer are apologias composed, no longer is anyone sentenced and condemned for such-and-such reasons. Everything is now illuminated by a transcendent light bringing out in the whole drama a sense and meaning that has escaped the very actors in the tragedy. The liturgical discourse, the discourse of worship, imposes a particular order, possesses its own grammar, and concentrates on one line of approach: the profession of faith in and the celebration of the presence of the savior, the suffering just one, now in truth the one raised up from the dead, the living one.

GUIDING INTEREST OF OUR READING OF JESUS' PASSION

As we have seen, the New Testament account of the passion of the Lord is profoundly marked by theological interpretations that were very relevant for its hearers and readers. They needed to justify this new figure of the messiah that they presented and preached—a suffering, crucified messiah. They had to demonstrate the unicity and the unity of God's plan, which was being carried out despite ruptures even as profound as that of the collapse of the historical project as envisioned by the messiah himself.

Not all these problems coincide precisely with our own. We are secure in the faith that Jesus is the Christ, and that the one who was crucified is the same historical being as the risen one. The crucified one is the living one. The context in which we read the scriptures and subject them to theological reflection is not only a liturgical context, a context of worship; we also discover a new meaning in the passion and death of the Lord, from a point of departure in a political commitment and within a liberative praxis. Our *Sitz im Leben,* our situation in life, then, is different. And this difference must be kept carefully in mind, for it permits another reading. It contemplates reality with other eyes. And yet the fonts are the same: the Gospels, written though these be within the parameters of another guiding interest, another key, another vital context. If the evangelists had had a liberative political interest, surely they would have written the Gospels very differently, and underscored other aspects of Christ's passion.

The evangelists do not attempt a profane reading of the drama of the passion. Everything is read *religiously*—that is, everything is kept in explicit reference to God. God enters directly into history. Hence the *historical* causes of Christ's death will be deeply hidden by the gospels. The Jews' rejection of Jesus, their stratagems, will be seen as a hardening of their hearts, a refusal to hear the voice of God speaking through Jesus. The political dimension—the interests of the status quo, the concern for the national security of Palestine—are not very clearly or explicitly set forth. Everything is subsumed in a transcendent, religious view of things.

Our interest, sprung from an experience of oppression, resistance, and liberation, is directed toward the detection of the causes of the failure of Jesus' project of liberation, the reasons, of a religio-political order, leading to his trial and liquidation. This interest of ours does not militate against a religious, transcendent meaning of the passion and death of the Lord, but only seeks to supply the dimension constituted by the historical, political mediations—in fine, the underpinnings—of that religious, transcendent meaning. We must not forget that Jesus did not die in bed. He was sentenced to execution and violently eliminated. Human responsibility played a role. It was not a drama with God as sole actor and sole agent. There was intrigue, there was conflict, there were agents giving bribes, there was imprisonment and torture. A sentence was drawn up, and executed on a cross. On this infrastructure, a theological interpretation was built and God's revelation was bestowed. But we cannot rest content with this interpretation, or with the facts recorded within the context of this interpretation. Probably all the facts, in their political dimension and conflictual entanglement, were present to the Jewish Christians of the primitive church. But these persons were guided by a religious, apologetic interest, and they recorded only those facts that fell within the framework of their religious interpretation.

A consequence of this observation is that a reading situated outside the direct interest of the New Testament accounts will have to take on the task of an antecedent critique. It will have to maintain ongoing vigilance vis-à-vis the scope of the New Testament interpretation and the historical reality of the facts narrated. It will have to ask itself in all honesty: To what extent are the facts as narrated the projection of an antecedent theological interpretation? To what extent do they constitute interpretations rather than events that actually occurred? And at the same time we shall have to ask ourselves at all times: To what extent does our own interest attempt to force the text to say more than it really says? To what extent are we projecting rather than assimilating? In the New Testament accounts, fact and interpretation form a homogeneous reality. This is what we have as a literary text. In view of our guiding interest, which is different from that of the New Testament, we must attempt to isolate the fact of the interpretation to which it has been subjected by the primitive church and recorded by the evangelists. Only in this way will our own reading, which is also intended to be theological, be possible. Let us, then, seek only to do this: place ourselves in the situation in which the evangelists found themselves. Like them, let us, too, proceed to a theological interpretation of the Lord's passion. Our attitude of faith is the same. Only the *Sitz im Leben*—the situation in life, the vital context—will be different.

Chapter 2

Jesus' Death as Consequence of a Praxis and a Message

In its *ontological* aspect, human death belongs to life itself. It is more than life's final moment. It is part and parcel of the very structure of life. Human life is structurally mortal. The moment we begin to live, we begin to die. And we continue to die, moment after moment, as our life goes on, until at last our dying is complete. And so we can speak adequately of death only if we speak of mortal life itself. In the ontological sense, then, we see, we can identify, death as the last moment of mortal life only if we understand death as a process moving toward completion all through our life, and finally reaching its perfection in life's last moment. The meaning of one's life is the meaning of one's death. And the meaning of one's death is the meaning of one's life.

In the *historical* aspect of Jesus' death, however, the termination of life was not the final stage of a natural development. It did not emerge as the termination of vital energy. The termination was introduced violently, by historical forces. Jesus' death was caused by a will interposed among the natural mechanisms. And this will, which caused death, consisted in a violent re-action to Jesus' action. What is important, then, is not so much the reaction, but Jesus' action, which provoked the contrary action of the physical liquidation of the agent. In other words Jesus' death can be understood only from a point of departure in his historical praxis, in his message, in the demands he makes and the conflicts he arouses.

In view of all of this, let us now consider:

1. Jesus' historical project
    a. The infrastructure of his time: the challenges
    b. The historical project (his message): the response
    c. Jesus' new praxis, liberating oppressed life
    d. Basis of the historical project and liberative praxis: the experience of God as Father

9

2. Jesus' violent death (chap. 3, below)
   a. Steps along a path
   b. Jesus' trial and sentencing
   c. Jesus' crucifixion

JESUS' HISTORICAL PROJECT

Before embarking upon our examination of Jesus' historical project, we must recover the historical concreteness of the person himself—this Jew called Jesus of Nazareth. The Jesus with whom we are familiar is Jesus Christ, eternal Son of God, lord of the universe, savior of the world, firstborn of all creation and firstfruits of resurrection among his many brothers and sisters. But these titles of honor and glorification conceal the lowly origins and historical trajectory of the real Jesus who walked among the people, moving through the villages of Galilee and finally dying ignominiously outside the walls of Jerusalem.

The person of faith, the ordinary reader of the Gospels, tends to consider Jesus' condition as God and savior as a primary, self-evident reality, a basic datum of which the apostles were aware right from the start. Jesus' activity is presented in the Gospels as crystalized, and absolutely consistent. He seems to know and foresee all things in advance. And indeed, was he not the eternal son of God? How easily, how searingly, his words flowed from his lips—for he was the eternal Word, in self-communication. Everything seems so easy, both the words and the deeds. Jesus had no options set before him, no decisions to make. Everything had been decided in advance, in the Father's eternal plan. Jesus was but the faithful executor of this plan.

This view of Jesus is dogmatic, not historical. It is the perspective of those who came after the fact, not of those who knew him before and during the fact.This is the interpretation of the disciples of the apostles, not that of the apostles.

The Jesus the apostles knew was Jesus of Nazareth, a prophet to whom they had joined their life and lot. Only slowly, and only from a point of departure in the resurrection, did it dawn on them who this Jesus really was—what mystery lay hidden beneath the fragility of this prophet of the people. In order to come to the point where they could say that he was the Christ-Messiah, the savior of the world, the Son of God, the firstborn of all creation, they had to travel a long, difficult path of prayer and reflection.

The Jesus of the apostles' daily experience is not the Jesus who is architect of the reign of God, who knows the plan perfectly a priori, the engineer with the whole, detailed blueprint in his pocket so that all he has to do is follow it to the tiniest detail. Their Jesus is a Jesus who searches, who prays, who is faced with a variety of options, who is tried and tempted, who feels pressured to make choices, who withdraws to the wasteland to learn the will of God, who gradually develops his overall project and then moves on to concrete options. All is fraught with danger, groping, preparation, growth, and gradual development. Not without reason does Saint Luke say, "Jesus . . . progressed steadily in wisdom and age and grace before God and men" (Luke 2:52; cf. 2:40). He says not "before men" only, as if little by little Jesus had revealed to human beings what he had always known because he was in God, but that he progressed "before God" as well. Little by little, step by step, Jesus came to know God's design and accept it to the hilt.

Jesus was genuinely a *homo viator,* like any one of ourselves, excepting that which makes us God's enemies, sin. He shared in the condition of every Jew of his time, especially that of Galileans, with their bad reputation as persons who associated with the pagans who lived in their land.

We believe in the mystery of the incarnation of God in Jesus of Nazareth. But this incarnation must not be emptied of content. Our belief in the incarnation must not be at the expense of Jesus' genuine humanity. It was not in spite of that humanity, but precisely in that humanity, that God was revealed. The divine project in Jesus did not destroy, but rather exalted, the human project of Jesus. The projects interpenetrate, in intimate union but without confusion, without absorption of the one by the other. The incarnation is not something merely passive, it is something profoundly active. God took on the life of Jesus, from its conception onward, as that life developed and assumed its decisive options. Jesus, in turn, was led to open himself to God, and he did so more and more.

It is within this framework of understanding that I propose to contextualize Jesus' historical project. "Project" here means fundamental option: the basic decision marking the orientation of one's life, determining one's ideas (theory) and practices, molding one's overall way of regarding the future. Any pro-ject, as the philological meaning suggests, has a dimension essentially bearing upon the future: *pro-* means "forward" and *-ject* means "to cast, to throw." How did Jesus represent to himself the future of the world? How did he act to concretize this representation? What were the reactions of the various social strata as they were affected by his preaching and activity? How did Jesus assimilate the conflict stirred up by those in power, those who prescribed the ideology of the time and place?

Infrastructure of Jesus' Time: The Challenges

The socio-political situation of Jesus' time contains surprising parallels with the situation from which the Latin American theology of liberation has emerged. Let us examine certain elements of this parallel:

General Regime of Dependency
For centuries, Palestine had been living in a situation of oppression. Since 587 B.C. the territory had been dependent on the great surrounding empires: Babylon (until 538), Persia (until 331), Alexander of Macedon (until 323) and his successors (the Ptolomeys of Egypt until 197 and the Seleucids of Syria until 166)—finally falling within the sphere of influence of Roman imperialism

(from 64 B.C.). Now Palestine was a little canton of the Roman province of Syria, governed at the time of Jesus' birth by a pagan king, Herod, with the support of the center, Rome. This dependency upon a center situated abroad was internalized by the presence of an army of occupation and a whole social class of tax collectors for the empire. The tax-collecting franchise was sold in Rome (by the equestrian class) to a group of Jews who, in their homeland, would sublet it to others, thus maintaining a network of itinerant functionaries. Extortion and exorbitant assessments were the order of the day. There were also the Sadducees, who played the Romans' game in order to maintain their huge capital investments, especially in the temple and the other large buildings of Jerusalem.

Political dependence meant cultural dependence. Educated in Rome, Herod pursued pharaonic construction projects—palaces, baths, theaters, fortresses. The presence of a pagan culture, the Roman, rendered the oppression all the more odious and humiliating, given the Jews' religious penchant.

Socio-economic Oppression

Palestinian economy was based on farming and fishing. Galilean society, the scene of Jesus' principal activity, was built of groups of small farmers or associations of fishermen. Generally there was work for everyone. The quality of life was not high. There was no system of savings, so that a famine or a major epidemic would provoke an exodus from the countryside to the towns in a search for work. Day workers would crowd the village squares (see Matt. 20:1–15), or would place themselves in the service of a large landholder in the hope of somehow attaining solvency. Because the Mosaic law awarded the firstborn male double the patrimony of the others, the wage-earning class gradually swelled its ranks to the point where its members might fail to find work and became genuine proletarians, beggars, vagabonds, or robbers. Wealthy landholders plundered the peasantry by moneylending, expropriating collateral in compensation for unpaid debts. The tax system was onerous and complex. Practically everything was taxed: each member of the family, and then land, livestock, fruits and grains, water, meat, salt and, especially, all roads. Herod's monumental construction projects had impoverished not only the common people but also the large landowners.

Jesus' hereditary occupation was that of a *tekton*—a carpenter or roofer. On occasion, a *tekton* might work as a stonemason. Saint Joseph was probably employed in the rebuilding of Seforis, a town on the other side of the Nazareth hills that the Romans had razed to the ground on the occasion of its occupation by Zealot guerrillas in the year 7 B.C.

The presence of foreign, pagan forces constituted a genuine religious temptation for the Jewish people. God was considered, and worshiped as, the sole ruler of the country and the people. God had repeatedly promised the people perpetual possession of the land of Israel. The current oppression inflamed the religious fantasy of many. Practically all thought that the situation would end soon, and expected it to come in the form of a spectacular divine intervention.

The air was charged with an apocalypticism from which, as the Gospels attest (see Mark 13 and parallels), Jesus himself was not entirely immune. A number of liberation movements, particularly those of the Zealots, sought to prepare for, or even hasten by provocative violence, God's salvific irruption, which would mean the liquidation of all the enemies of Israel and the subjection of all peoples to the absolute sovereignty of Yahweh.

Religious Oppression

The deepest oppression, however, was not owing to the presence of a foreign, pagan power, but emerged from a legalistic interpretation of religion and of the will of God. Observance of the Mosaic law had become the very essence of postexilic Judaism. Sophistical interpretations and absurd traditions had caused the law to degenerate into a terrible slavery, imposed in the name of God (Matt. 23:4; Luke 11:46). Jesus fairly exploded: "You have made a fine art of setting aside God's commandment in the interests of keeping your traditions!" (Mark 7:9).

A scrupulous observance of the law, in the interest of ensuring one's salvation, had made the people forget God, the author of the law and of salvation. The Pharisees were particularly observant of the letter of the law, and terrorized the people with the same scrupulosity. The Pharisees contemptuously referred to the people as "this lot, that knows nothing about the Law," and dismissed them as "lost" (John 7:49). Legally the Pharisees were letter-perfect. But underneath lurked a fundamental wickedness, and Jesus tore away their disguise: "You pay tithes on mint and herbs and seeds while neglecting the weightier matters of the Law, justice and mercy and good faith" (Matt. 23:23).

Instead of furthering liberation, the law had become a prison with golden bars. Instead of being an aid to human beings in the encounter with their fellows and with God, the law shut them off from both, discriminating between those whom God loved and those whom God did not love, between the pure and the impure, between my neighbor whom I should love and my enemy whom I may hate. The Pharisees had a morbid conception of God. Their God no longer spoke to human beings. Their God had left them a Law.

Jesus' Historical Project: The Answer

An Absolute Meaning that Contests the Present

Jesus' reaction to this state of affairs is a bit surprising. He does not come forward as a revolutionary committed to modify the prevailing power structure, like a Bar Kochba. Nor does he rise up as a preacher interested only in the conversion of consciences, like a Saint John the Baptist. No, he proclaims an ultimate, structural, all-embracing meaning, one that transcends everything that is feasible and determinable by human beings. He proclaims an ultimate end, one that calls into question social, political, and religious interests. Jesus maintains this universal, cosmic perspective in everything that he says and does. He does not immediately satisfy the concrete, limited expectations of his audience. Rather he summons his hearers to an absolutely transcendent dimension, a dimension that overflows the narrow confines of this world in its historical factuality as the locus of the interplay of powers and interests, the stage set for the dramatic struggle for the survival of the fittest. He does not proclaim a particular, political, economic, religious meaning—but an absolute, all-comprehending, all-transcending meaning. His watchword, his key concept, is charged with radical meaning: he proclaims the "reign of God."

This is an expression that goes straight to a human being's most profound utopian depths. Jesus strikes a taut string, and dynamisms of absolute hope, which had lain dormant or had been crushed by historical structures, ring out in reply. He awakens a sleeping hope of total liberation from everything that alienates men and women from their true identity. In his inaugural discourse itself he articulates this utopian dream, and the promise he makes is that this dream will now be glorious reality: "This is the time of fulfillment. The reign of God is at hand! Reform your lives and believe in the gospel!" (Mark 1:15).

It is creation in all its dimensions that will be liberated, not just the small world of the Jews of that time and place. But even this is not what is special about Jesus' message. Jesus' announcement is more than just another in a long series of prophetic, utopian proclamations with which his hearers were only too familiar. Jewish and pagan prophets of all times had proclaimed the coming of a new world of total reconciliation. So far, then, Jesus demonstrates no originality. What is new with Jesus is that he actually anticipates the future: he renders the utopian "topian," topical, localized, concretized. He does not say simply, "the reign of god will come." He says, "the reign of God is at hand" (Mark 1:15; cf. Matt. 4:17), "is already in your midst" (Luke 17:21). With Jesus' presence, the reign of God is actually present: "If it is by the finger of God that I cast out devils, then the reign of God is upon you" (Luke 11:20). In Jesus, the mightier one who vanquishes the less mighty is here at last (see Mark 3:27).

Jesus' Temptation: To Regionalize the Reign of God

The "reign of God" stands for the totality of meaning of the world in God. The temptation is to regionalize it, "privatize" it, reduce it to intrahuman dimensions. Liberation is real liberation only when it is universal, all-comprehensive—when it is a translation of the absolute meaning that is the object of every human being's quest. Hence a regionalization of the reign of liberation in terms of some ideology of commonweal, or in terms of a religious ideology, is tantamount to perverting the original meaning of the reign of God in Jesus' intention.

Jesus, the Gospels tell, faced this very temptation (Matt. 4:1–11; Luke 4:1–13). It remained with him throughout his life (Luke 22:28). It consisted precisely in the temptation to reduce the universality inherent in the authentic concept of the reign of God to the dimensions of a province of this world, the temptation to concretize that reign in the form of (1) political domination (the temptation on the mountain, whence Jesus could look out on all the kingdoms of the world), (2) religious power (the temptation on the pinnacle of the temple), or (3) the reign of what we might style the "social and political miraculous," which attempts to satisfy basic needs of human beings like hunger (the temptation to change stones into bread). These three temptations of power correspond precisely to the three models of the reign of God and of the messiah in vogue in the expectations of the time. The messiah would be a prophet, a priest, and a king. But all three models are models of power.

Christ is tempted his whole life long to use the divine power available to him to impose by force, by a feat of magic, a radical transformation on this world. The difficulty is that this would be tantamount to a manipulation of the human will. It would have constituted a dispensation from human responsibilities. Men and women would be spectators and beneficiaries, but not participants. They would not make history. They would be liberated paternalistically: liberation would not be the result of a human undertaking.

Jesus determinedly refuses to establish a reign of power. He is the servant, not the dominator, of every human creature. It is God's love, then, not God's power, that Jesus incarnates. Still better, Jesus renders visible precisely the power of God's love, which is the power to establish an order that does not violate human liberty, does not exempt human beings from their duty to take their own project in hand. This is why the inauguration of the reign of God in history is through conversion. Through conversion, human beings, in the very act of welcoming the novelty of new hope for this world, cooperate in its renovation, by what they build in the way of political, social, religious, and personal mediations.

In all his attitudes, whether in the moral disputes with the Pharisees or in the temptation to distribute power among his own apostles (Luke 9:46–48; Matt. 20:20–28), Jesus always refuses to dictate particularizing norms. He always refuses to formulate solutions or foster hopes that would regionalize the reign of God. Thereby he takes his critical distance from the structure that constitutes the mainstay of our world: power as domination.

Jesus' refusal to have recourse to power turns the masses away from him in disappointment. Only had they seen his power would they have believed: "Let's see him come down from that cross and then we will believe in him" (Matt. 27:42). Power as a religious and liberative category is completely "de-divinized" by Jesus. Power as domination is essentially diabolical—totally contrary to the mystery of God (Matt. 4:1–11; Luke 4:1–13).

Jesus' unshakable attachment to preserving the character of God's reign as universal and total does not, however, incline him to sit back and do nothing about it—simply wait for the dazzling arrival of the new order. With Jesus, the absolute end is mediated in concrete deeds. It is anticipated by surprising behavior; it is rendered viable in attitudes signifying that the end is already present, in the midst of life.

Thus the liberation effectuated by Jesus Christ is composed of two elements. First, it is the total liberation of all history, not merely of certain of its segments. Second and concomitantly, it anticipates this totality in a liberative process concretized in partial liberations—liberations always open to this totality. On the one hand he proclaims total hope on the level of the utopian future. On the other hand he renders that hope viable in the present. If he were to preach the utopia of a favorable end and outcome for humankind without anticipating that outcome in history, he would be fostering fantasies, encouraging harmless phantasmagorias devoid of credibility. If he were to introduce partial liberations bereft of all perspective of totality and future, he would be frustrating the hopes he had aroused, and thereby fall into an "immediatism" devoid of substance. Jesus maintains a dialectical tension: the reign of God is already in our midst, the new order is already fermenting, and yet—and yet it is still future, the object of hope, and of the common enterprise of all humankind and God.

To Deliver the Human Being from an Oppressed Life: Jesus' New Praxis

The reign of God, the eschatological liberation of the world, is already in process, then, is already being established in history. It takes shape in concrete modifications of actual life. Let us single out some of the concrete steps by which the new world is anticipated in the redemptive, liberating process of which Jesus Christ is the agent.

Relativization of Human Self-sufficiency

In the world as Jesus found it, human beings were enslaved by certain absolutizations. They were under the yoke of the absolutization of religion, of tradition, and of the law.

Religion was no longer the way in which human beings expressed their openness to God. It had crystalized and stagnated in a world of its own, a world of rites and sacrifices. Jesus takes his place in the prophetical tradition when he says that love, justice, and mercy are more important than official worship (Mark 7:6-8). The criteria of salvation are not to be sought in the sphere of cultic worship. They are found in the love of one's neighbor. There is something more important than the Sabbath and human tradition: human beings (Mark 2:23-26). Human beings are worth more than anything else in the world (Matt. 6:26), more central and more compelling than worship (Luke 10:30-37) or sacrifice (Matt. 5:23-24; Mark 12:33). Human beings take precedence over piety and the observance of the sacred prescriptions of the law and tradition (Matt. 23:23). Whenever Jesus speaks of the love of God, he speaks of the love of neighbor in the same breath (Mark 12:31-33; Matt. 22:36-39 and parallels). It is in one's love of one's neighbor, and not in God as God, that salvation is decided (Matt. 25:31-46). When someone asks what can be done to reach salvation, Jesus answers by reciting the commandments of the second table, all of which refer to our neighbor (Mark 10:17-22).

Clearly, then, we may not speak of God abstractly—prescinding from God's daughters and sons, prescinding from the love we owe our fellow human beings. There is a oneness between love for neighbor and love for God. Saint John conveys this oneness very well:

> If anyone says, "My love is fixed on God,"
> yet hates his brother,
> he is a liar.
> One who has no love for the brother he has seen
> cannot love the God he has not seen [1 John 4:20].

This is how Jesus "de-absolutizes" the cultic, legal, and religious forms that had come to monopolize all routes to salvation. Salvation comes by way of our neighbor. The purpose of religion is not to substitute for our neighbor, but to establish in us a permanent orientation to genuine love of the other—in whom, incognito, God is hidden (Mark 6:20–21; Matt. 25:40). The relativization effectuated by Jesus extends to the sacred power of the Caesars, whose divine character he denies (Matt. 22:21). Caesar may claim to be the last instance— but "you would have no power over me whatever unless it were given you from above," Jesus retorts to Pilate (John 19:11).

Creation of a New Solidarity

However, redemption goes beyond a relativization of laws and forms of official worship. Redemption is also incarnated in a new kind of solidarity among human beings. The social world of Jesus' time was characterized by a very complex structure. This structuring included social discrimination between the clean and the unclean; between neighbor and nonneighbor; between Jews and pagans; between men and women; between theologians who observed the laws and a simple people terrorized in its oppressed conscience by its inability to live according to the legal interpretations of the doctors of the law; between Pharisees and the ritually unclean, the ostracized sick, and anyone reputed to be a sinner.

But Jesus enters into solidarity with all the oppressed. He takes sides with the weak, with all those criticized on the basis of the established canons: the prostitute, the Samaritan heretic, the tax collector, the Roman centurion, the person blind from birth, the paralytic, the hunchback, the pagan Syro-Phoenician, the apostles when they are criticized for not fasting after the manner of the disciples of John. Jesus makes everyone welcome. All are made to understand that they are not outside the pale of salvation, but that God loves everyone, even "the ungrateful and the wicked" (Luke 6:35), for those "who are healthy do not need a doctor; sick people do" (Mark 2:17). This is why Jesus' task is "to search out and save what is lost" (Luke 19:10).

Jesus has no fear of the consequences of his solidarity with the outcast. He is vilified, insulted, accused of keeping bad company, labeled subversive, heretical, possessed, insane, and more. But this is the love, and the kind of mediation, by which one learns the meaning of the reign of God, and of liberation from the structures of oppression that discriminate between human being and human being. My neighbor is not my fellow believer, or a person of my race, or a member of my family. My neighbor is any person at all, from the moment I approach that person, regardless of his or her ideology or religious profession (see Luke 10:30–37).

Respect for the Freedom of Others

As we read the Gospels and observe Jesus' manner of preaching, we are immediately struck by the fact that he never speaks in a supercilious, authoritarian tone. His language is simple, full of parables and examples taken from the everyday life of the times. He mingles with the masses, he listens, he asks questions. He gives individuals a chance to express their own mind. He asks the inquirer what the law says, he questions the disciples as to what others say about him, he asks the sufferer by the roadside what he hopes for. He allows the Samaritan at the well to speak her mind. He listens to the Pharisees' questions. He does not give systematic instruction after the manner of a schoolteacher, he answers questions, he offers persons the opportunity to define themselves, gives them the freedom to take a position on matters crucial to their own destiny. When questioned about taxes—that is, about Caesar's political power—he holds no theoretical disquisitions; he simply requests that he be brought the coin of tribute and he inquires whose coin it is. He always gives the other person an opportunity to speak. Only the rich youth does not have his say. Perhaps this is why we do not know his name—he did not define himself.

Jesus refuses to allow himself to be served by others. He himself serves at table (Luke 22:27). Here we have none of the mystification of humility that we see in church history whenever popes and bishops have made themselves into masters instead of being servants. They call themselves servants, but often enough this was merely their way of camouflaging a power that ran counter to the gospel, a power that oppressed consciences. Jesus' insistence on the character of power as service, and on the last being first (Mark 10:42–44; 9:35; Matt. 28:8–12), is an attempt to do away with the ruler-slave relationship, power structured in terms of blind submission, a structure of privileges. Jesus preaches not *hierarchia*—sacred power—but *hierodoulia:* sacred service. The power Jesus proclaims is not an autocratic power, sufficient unto itself, but a service in function of the community.

No authority, not even an ecclesiastical authority, that asserts itself independently of the community of the faithful can lay claim to a share in Jesus' authority. This was how Jesus himself behaved. His argumentation is never fanatical, never demands passive submission to its assertions. He attempts only to persuade, to state his argument clearly, to appeal to good sense and reason. His assertions are not "authoritative," but persuasive. He always leaves the other a space for freedom. His disciples are not instilled with a fanaticism for their doctrine, but with respect even for enemies and opponents. Jesus never employs violence to make his ideas prevail. He appeals to, and speaks to, consciences. His intimates, the twelve, include a collaborator with the occupying forces, a tax collector (Mark 2:15–17), and even a nationalist Zealot guerrilla (Mark 3:18–19), coexisting, and forming a community with Jesus, despite the tensions we observe among its enthusiasts and skeptics.

An Inexhaustible Capacity to Bear up under Conflict

I am attempting to demonstrate how, in the concrete, Christ redeems and liberates along the actual pathways of concrete history. He addresses all. He discriminates against no one. "No one who comes will I ever reject, " he says in Saint John. Here we have a paradigmatic expression of Jesus' attitude.

First and foremost, however, he addresses his evangelization to the poor— and not just to the economically needy:

> The poor are the oppressed in the broadest sense: those who suffer
> oppression and cannot defend themselves, the hopeless, those who have
> no salvation . . . all who suffer need, the hungry, the thirsty, the naked,
> the homeless, the stranger, the sick, the imprisoned, the overburdened,
> the last, the simple, the lost, and sinners [Jeremias, *Teología,* 138].

Jesus seeks to help all these persons, striving to defend their rights, especially in the case of the sick, lepers, or the possessed, who were considered public sinners and were calumniated as such. Jesus takes up the defense of their rights, then, demonstrating that not all illness is the result of sin, whether personal or that of one's forebears, nor does it render its victims impure.

He often moves in the circles of his legalistic, conservative opponents, who are caught up in the pursuit of honor, as are the Pharisees (Mark 2:13–3:6). He accepts invitations to dine with them (Luke 7:36–50; 11:37–52), but fails to share their mentality. "Woe to you rich," he says, "for your consolation is now" (Luke 6:24). He also accepts invitations from tax collectors, despite their evil reputation, and his presence among them transforms their behavior, as the story of Zacchaeus shows.

Everything in our hearts or in our society that can constitute an assault on the rights of others is condemned by Christ: hatred, anger (Matt. 5:21–22), jealousy (Matt. 5:27–28), calumny, aggression, murder. Jesus argues for goodness and gentleness, and criticizes any lack of respect for the dignity of others (Matt. 7:1–15; Luke 6:37–41). He walks his path, not with prideful distance from the human conflict, but "getting involved," taking sides whenever there is a question of defending the rights of another, be that other a heretic, pagan, or stranger, someone with a bad reputation, a woman, or a child, a public sinner, someone ill, or someone marginalized. He communicates with all, and appeals for the renunciation of violence as an instrument for the attainment of one's objectives.

It is of the essence of self-serving power to seek after ever more power, and to strive to subjugate others to one's own views and notions. Then there is fear, revenge, and the will to domination, all of which burst human communion asunder. The resultant human order is created by imposition, and at great social cost. Any questioning of the status quo, any threat to security, any suggestion of a change in the established order, whether in civil or religious society, is swept away, thanks to a rigorous system of surveillance. When a threat to the established order begins to have real effects, primitive mechanisms of calumny, hatred, repression, and elimination are set in motion. The order must be cleansed of the enemies of security. And we actually hear those who are guilty of this attitude and these procedures appealing to the name of Jesus Christ in order to justify themselves, whereas Jesus' attitudes were calculated to generate a process of reflection, change, and frank communication among groups.

Corresponding to the appeal for renunciation of power is an appeal for forgiveness and mercy. This presupposes a keen perception of the reality of the world. There will always be structures of power and revenge. They must not be the occasion of discouragement, still less of emulation. Here we see the need for forgiveness, mercy, and the patience to bear up under and live with the excesses committed by power. And so Jesus commands us to love our enemies. Now, loving our enemies does not mean loving them romantically, as if they were simply another kind of friend. Loving our enemies means loving them *as* enemies, and this means, first of all, discovering that they are enemies, and then loving them as Jesus loved his enemies. Jesus did not shun communication with his enemies, but challenged the attitudes that enslaved them and made them enemies. Renunciation of the structures and machinations of hatred is not the same as renunciation of opposition. Jesus opposed, disputed, argued—but not in accompaniment with the use of violence: he did all this in a profound commitment to persons. To renounce opposition would be to renounce a neighbor's good and the defense of his or her rights, so that we would simply be adding fuel to the fire of domination.

Acceptance of Mortality

In Jesus' life we see life as it is, with all its contradictions. Jesus is not a complainer, wandering about weeping over all the evil that there is in the world. "Surely God could have made a better world! How much sin and evil there is in human beings! Why doesn't God do something about it?" Nothing of this do we find in Jesus. Jesus takes life as he finds it. He does not refuse the sacrifice that every truly committed life includes: isolation, persecution, misunderstanding, libel, and all the rest. He accepts all human limitations. Everything that is authentically human is seen in Jesus: anger, joy, kindness, sorrow, temptation, poverty, hunger, thirst, compassion, and longing. He lives life as a gift, and not as a long, continuous exercise in self-devotion (Mark 10:42-45): "The Son of Man has come not to be served but to serve" (v. 45). He knows no vacillations in his fundamental attitude: that of living always as a being-for-others.

But to live life as gift is to live it as sacrifice. To live life as gift is to spend it in behalf of others. If death is not merely the final moment of life, but part and parcel of the structure of life, inasmuch as mortal life ebbs away, moment by moment, slowly emptying, dying, from the moment it is conceived—and if death as this gradual emptying is more than just biological fatality, but an opportunity for persons to accept, in liberty, the finitude and mortality of life, and thus open themselves to something greater than death—if to die, then, is to make room for something larger, if to die is to empty oneself in order to receive the fullnesss of the advent of the one who is greater than life—then we can say that the life of Christ, from its first moment, was an acceptance of death, with all the courage and mettle of which anyone is capable. Jesus was completely empty of himself, so that he could be full of others and God. He accepted mortal life, accepted the death that hung like a dark cloud over his commitment to the life of itinerant prophet and the messiah who rescues human beings. This is the context in which we must reflect on the death of Christ and its redemptive meaning.

We are accustomed to hearing the account of Jesus' death in the form that we have it in the passion narratives. There it is clear that his death was for our sins. We see that it occurred in fulfillment of the prophecies of the Old Testament, and that it was part of the divine mission entrusted to Jesus by the Father, so that, in the salvific plan of God, this death had to be. These interpretations bring out the *transcendent* truth of Jesus' total self-bestowal, his total surrender—but they can lead us to misunderstand the genuine *historical* reality of the final lot of Jesus Christ.

Actually these gospel interpretations are the end product of a lengthy process of reflection undertaken by the primitive Christian community regarding the scandal of Good Friday. In Jesus' ignominious death on the cross (Gal. 3:13)—the sign par excellence, in those days, of God's abandonment of a false prophet (and here it is important to examine Matt. 27:39–44; Mark 15:29–32; Luke 23:35–37)—the first Christians faced an enormous problem. In the light of the resurrection, and of a rereading of and meditation on the Old Testament scriptures (see Luke 24:13–35), what before had been absurd they suddenly began to see as perfectly intelligible. This interpretive, theological work, this discovery of a secret meaning underlying the ignominious facts of the passion, was incorporated into the biblical accounts of the trial, passion, death, and resurrection of Jesus Christ. The evangelists did not work as neutral historians. They were theologians, with a theological concern: the transcendent, universal, definitive meaning of the death of Christ.

This kind of interpretation, however valid in itself, easily inclines the unwary reader to create an image of the passion as some manner of suprahistorical drama, in which the actors—Jesus, the Jews, Judas, Pilate—appear on stage like puppets playing a scene written for them beforehand, and thus exempt from any personal initiative and responsibility. Jesus' death no longer appears in its traumatic, afflicting aspect. After all, Jesus, too, is merely executing a foreordained plan. The need for this plan, however, is left unclear. Jesus' death is dissociated from the rest of his life and begins to take on a salvific meaning of its own. And thereby much of the historical dimension of Jesus' death is lost. That death was the consequence of Jesus' behavior, of his lofty attitudes. Jesus, we must remember, was sentenced to death in a courtroom. Catholic theologian Christian Duquoc is correct when he says:

In reality, Jesus' passion is inseparable from his earthly life, from his word. It is not only his resurrection, but his life, as well, that gives meaning to his death. Jesus did not die a casual death. He was sentenced to die not out of some misunderstanding or other—but by reason of his actual, daily, historical attitude. A reading that leaps at once from the particularity of this life and this death to a "metaphysical" conflict between love and hate, between disbelief and belief in the Son of God, is oblivious of the multiplicity of mediations necessary to an understanding of this life and this death. A like neglect of history has religious consequences. As an example, meditation on the passion and death of Jesus is not, as we know, always without overtones of morbidity. Instead of teaching us to repulse evil and death, a traditional meditation on the passion of Christ often produces an unhealthy fixation, a resignation. Suffering and death are glorified in themselves [Duquoc, *Jesus, homem,* 197].

The *timeless* meaning of the death of Christ, as discovered by the primitive community, recorded in the Gospels, and altogether valid, should be extracted from this *historical* context of that death, rather than from a theological one. Only thus will that meaning cease to be ahistorical, and at bottom empty and vacuous. And only thus will it acquire genuinely valid dimensions for contemporary faith as well.

In the first place, the death of Christ was human. In other words, we find it in the context of a life, a life of conflict, a life in which death did not come by imposition from without, by divine decree, but was inflicted by particular human beings. Indeed, this is why this death can be historically followed and recounted.

Jesus died for the reasons any prophet ever dies. He placed a higher value on the principles he preached than on his own life. He preferred to die freely rather than renounce truth, justice, human rights, the ideal of a universal communion of sisters and brothers, the truth of the human condition as that of sons and daughters of God, and the unlimited goodness of God the Father. On this level, Christ joins the host of the thousands of witnesses who have preached the betterment of this world and the creation of a human society more marked by a communion of brothers and sisters and by greater openness to the Absolute. Jesus' death is a protest against closed, installed systems, and a permanent indictment of the way this world closes in upon itself—the very definition of sin.

Christ's death had been in process all his life long. The reflections I have sketched above show that the Jesus phenomenon constituted a radical crisis in the Judaism of his time. Jesus comes forward as a prophet proclaiming not "tradition," but a new teaching (Mark 1:27)—a prophet who does not simply preach the observance of the law and its interpretations, but who behaves as sovereign in their regard: if the law is a help to love and to the encounter of human beings with one another and with God, Jesus embraces the law; but if it is an obstacle to the encounter of the other and God, he skirts it or indeed abolishes it. The will of God, for the prophet from Nazareth, is not to be found in the *locus classicus* of scripture alone. Life itself is the locus of a manifestation of the salvific will of God in our regard. An obsession with the liberation of the oppressed conscience permeates all Jesus' attitudes and words. The crowds perceive it. They grow enthusiastic. The authorities are terrified: Jesus represents a threat to the established system of security, and might incite the masses against the Roman army of occupation. The authority with which he speaks and the sovereignty he assumes in his attitudes occasion a crisis of conscience for the mentors of official dogmatics. This fellow from Galilee is moving too far from official orthodoxy. He fails to justify his doctrine, his behavior, his demands, by any criterion known to the establishment.

We must not imagine that the Jews, the Pharisees, and the mentors of the social and religious order of the time were persons of unmitigated bad will— malevolent, vindictive, persecutive, ill-intentioned individuals bent on working any evil they could. No, they were faithful observers of the law, and of a religion piously handed down by generations before them, a religion that had counted martyrs and confessors. The questioning to which they subjected Jesus, their attempt to box him into the canons of established moral and dogmatic theology, sprang from the crisis of conscience that they themselves were experiencing, and that the personage and activity of Jesus had prompted. They were seeking to wall him up within a framework defined by the law. Failing this, they isolated him, calumniated him, put him on trial, sentenced him, and finally crucified him.

Christ's death resulted from a very concrete and circumstantial, altogether legally delineated, conflict. It was the fruit neither of a "sadistic mechanism" nor of a "judicial error." Jesus really looked to his adversaries like a false prophet, a disturber of the religious status quo, who might also disturb the political status quo. A system of values all locked up and self-contained, a system of values that had become untouchable and unquestionable, incapable of ever being opened up again so that something new could be learned, a system without any breadth of vision, and absolutely fanatical vis-à-vis the organization of life and religion, fraught with traditionalism, possessed of a self-sufficiency based exclusively on its own tradition and orthodoxy, and plagued with all the pettiness that even today often characterizes the defenders of an established order, be they clerics or politicians—generally with great good will, but bereft of any critical or historical sense—a system burdened with all these banal shortcomings, none of which by itself constitutes a serious crime, brought Jesus' life to an end.

Basis of a Historical Project and Liberative Praxis: Experience of God as Father

The picture I have just painted might seem too anthropological. I have spoken of a certain Galilean of times gone by who somehow liberated his fellow human beings by a remarkable life and death, like so many who had come before him and so many who would come after him. And indeed, on this level of our reflection, Jesus Christ simply takes his place in the "gallery of the just," the hall of fame of all the prophets who have ever been persecuted and murdered. As we shall see later, only his resurrection raises Jesus above all analogies and reveals new dimensions in the relative commonplaceness of his death as a martyred prophet.

Still, one really must ask: Whence sprang the force and vigor of that life of liberation?

The answer is clear from the Gospels themselves. Jesus' project of liberation sprang from a profound encounter with a God whom he experienced as, yes, the absolute meaning of all history, the God of the "reign of God"—but whom he experienced as a Father, too, a Father of infinite goodness and limitless love for all human beings, especially for the ungrateful and the wicked, the wandering and the lost. Jesus' experience is no longer that of a God of the law, discriminating between the good and the evil, the just and the unjust, but that of a good God, who loves and forgives, who goes in search of the lost sheep, who waits anxiously at the gate for the return of his prodigal child, and who rejoices more at the conversion of one sinner than at the salvation of ninety-nine just.

Ultimately, and in its deepest roots, Jesus' new praxis as I have sketched it above is based on this new experience of God. A person confident of being totally loved by God will love as God loves—indiscriminately, universally, with a love that embraces both friends and enemies. A person confident of being accepted by God, and forgiven by God, will accept and forgive others. Jesus incarnated the Father's love and forgiveness. He was good and merciful with all, especially with those rejected by religion and society. In Jesus, this was not "humanitarianism." It was the concretization of the Father's love in real life. If this is God's manner of dealing with everyone, why should it not be that of the Son of God?

Chapter 3

Jesus' Death as a Crime

Let us now attempt to trace the historical steps in Jesus' trial, sentence, and crucifixion. As noted above, the gospel texts as we have them are permeated with a theology, by which new meaning is given to the facts of Jesus' passion in the light of the resurrection. It is extremely difficult, if not to say downright problematic, simply to distinguish, in these texts, their historical content from their faith-inspired interpretation. Scholarly exegesis has bent valiant efforts in the attempt, but without producing much of a consensus.

Furthermore, readers not particularly familiar with the procedures of modern biblical exegesis—procedures duly sanctioned by the Second Vatican Council and accepted by the common practice of academicians—may often feel perplexed at the assertions that scientific exegesis feels safe in making. The decision of exegetes to accept one passage as historical while labeling another the product of theological reflection on the part of the evangelist and his particular community may seem excessively arbitrary. Actually, exegetical procedures are not as arbitrary as they might appear. They follow the rather well established rules for all historico-critical exegesis. Still, in view of the nature of the texts under consideration, a divergency of opinions in the questions facing us is scarcely surprising. The task is a difficult one, and the various opinions have their own exegetical and theological rationality.

We must also recognize that there is no such thing as a completely neutral exegesis. Exegetes read their texts with the eyes they have, and interpret them with the theologico-dogmatic presuppositions that they have in their heads and hearts, the heads and hearts of these particular human beings who believe in Jesus Christ as God incarnate and savior of the world. Underlying any exegetical undertaking is an antecedent image of Jesus, and this image necessarily governs and guides the investigation. It emerges from (1) the faith of the church, and Christian education, from childhood through graduate studies in theology, and (2) the exegete's own previous critical study of the texts of the New Testament. Whatever be the theologian's image of Jesus, that will be the theologian's guide in exegetical discussions. He or she will embrace this solution or that one, depending on which one "squares" best with his or her image of Jesus and comprehensive view of the christological mystery.

I say all this in order to warn the reader of the scope and limits of my own exposition. Mine will be one reading among many others, legitimate readings all, and familiar to popular piety and received theology as interpretations handed down through traditional ecclesial channels. But mine will be different from the others. May I repeat what was stated at the outset of this experiment. I do my reflection in a long christological tradition, that of Saint Francis and the great Franciscan doctors who, with tender simplicity and simple tenderness, reflected on the sacred humanity of Jesus in its most radical meaning as God's own annihilation and death on the cross. My particular reflection seeks to assimilate as well the findings of scholarly exegesis with respect to the gospel accounts of the passion, with a view to affording these findings the opportunity to fructify in their systematic, dogmatic aspect. I shall follow weighty authorities in the field of exegesis—Eduard Lohse, Heinz Schürmann, Josef Blinzler, Pierre Benoit, and others. I shall not rehearse their discussions; this would take us too far afield. I shall adopt their findings, however, whenever they appear to me to be sufficiently to the measure of the christological image that I here seek, in faith, to construct. But the reader should be aware that there are other exegetical conclusions as well, which pass by different routes, and they are equally legitimate and ecclesial. My own approach is intended to be of assistance to readers who desire to sound the depths of the humanity of Jesus Christ, that they may find there both a greater God and a nearer God, and that thereby they may feel themselves called to follow and imitate the same road and way of life that this Jesus trod and lived—Jesus the suffering, martyred Christ.

According to Ludger Schenke, who has carefully studied the literary evolution of the passion texts, the pre-Markan (oral) account of the passion must have been as follows (Schenke, 135–37). (Chapter and verse numbers refer to the text of Saint Mark's Gospel as we have it today.)

THE ORIGINAL PASSION ACCOUNT SUBSEQUENTLY AUGMENTED BY MARK

[Mark chap. 14] The feasts of Passover and Unleavened Bread were to be observed in two days' time (v. 1a). They went then to a place named Gethsemani (32a). Then [Jesus] began to be filled with fear and distress. He said to them, "My heart is filled with sorrow to the point of death. Remain here and stay awake" (34). He advanced a little and fell to the ground (35a). He kept saying, "*Abba,* Father, you have the power to do all things. Take this cup away from me. But let it be as you would have it, not as I" (36). When he returned he found them asleep. He said to Peter, "Asleep, Simon? You could not stay awake for even an hour? [37]. The spirit is willing but nature is weak" (38b). They could not keep their eyes open, nor did they know what to say to him (40b). [And he said to them,] "It will have to do [41b]. Rouse yourselves and come along. See! My betrayer is near" (42).

Even while he was still speaking, Judas, one of the Twelve, made his appearance accompanied by a crowd with swords and clubs; these people had been sent by the chief priests, the scribes, and the elders (43). The betrayer had arranged a signal for them, saying, "The man I shall embrace is the one; arrest him and lead him away, taking every precaution" (44). He then went directly over to him and said, "Rabbi!" and embraced him (45). At this, they laid hands on him and arrested him (46). One of the bystanders drew his sword and struck the high priest's slave, cutting off his ear (47). With that, all deserted him and fled (50).

Then they led Jesus off to the high priest (53a). The chief priests with the whole Sanhedrin were busy soliciting testimony against Jesus that would lead to his death, but they could not find any (55). Many spoke against him falsely under oath but their testimony did not agree (56). The high priest rose to his feet before the court and began to interrogate Jesus: "Have you no answer to what these men testify against you?" (60). But Jesus remained silent; he made no reply. Once again the high priest interrogated him: "Are you the Messiah, the Son of the Blessed One?" (61). Then Jesus answered: "I am" (62a). At that the high priest tore his robes and said: "What further need do we have of witnesses? [63]. You have heard the blasphemy. What is your verdict?" They all concurred in the verdict "guilty," with its sentence of death (64). Some of them then began to spit on him. They blindfolded him and hit him, saying, "Play the prophet!" while the officers manhandled him (65).

[Mark chap. 15] The chief priests, with the elders and scribes (that is, the whole Sanhedrin), reached a decision. They bound Jesus, led him away, and handed him over to Pilate (v. 1bc). [And the high priest made serious accusations against him.] Pilate interrogated him: "Surely you have some answer? See how many accusations they are leveling against you" (4). But greatly to Pilate's surprise, Jesus made no further response (5). And Pilate interrogated him [again]: "Are you the king of the Jews?" "You are the one who is saying it," Jesus replied (2).

After [Pilate] had had Jesus scourged, he handed him over to be crucified (15b). The soldiers now led Jesus away into the hall known as the praetorium; at the same time they assembled the whole cohort (16). They dressed him in royal purple, then wove a crown of thorns and put it on him (17), and began to salute him, "All hail! King of the Jews!" (18). Continually striking Jesus on the head with a reed and spitting at him, they genuflected before him and pretended to pay him homage (19). When they had finished mocking him, they stripped him of the purple, dressed him in his own clothes, and led him out to crucify him (20). They brought Jesus to the site of Golgotha (22a). They tried to give him wine drugged with myrrh, but he would not take it (23). Then they crucified him and divided up his garments by rolling dice for them to see what each should take (24). The inscription proclaiming his offense read "THE KING OF THE JEWS" (26). With him they crucified two insurgents, one at his right and one at his left (27). People going by kept insulting him, tossing their heads and saying, "Save yourself now by coming down from that cross! [30]. Let the

'Messiah, the king of Israel,' come down from that cross and now, so that we can see it and believe in him!" The men who had been crucified with him likewise kept taunting him (32).

[At the ninth hour] Jesus cried in a loud voice, *"Eloi, Eloi, lama sabach-thani?"* (34a). Someone ran off, and soaking a sponge in sour wine, stuck it on a reed to try to make him drink (36a). Then Jesus, uttering a loud cry, breathed his last (37). The centurion who stood guard over him, on seeing the manner of his death, declared, "Clearly this man was the Son of God!" (39).

[Because it was] the Preparation Day (42b), Joseph from Arimathea arrived—a distinguished member of the Sanhedrin. He was another who looked forward to the reign of God. He was bold enough to seek an audience with Pilate and urgently requested the body of Jesus (43). Pilate was surprised that Jesus should have died so soon. He summoned the centurion and inquired whether Jesus was already dead (44). Learning that from him that he was dead, Pilate released the corpse to Joseph (45). Then, having bought a linen shroud, Joseph took him down, wrapped him in the linen, and laid him in a tomb which had been cut out of rock (46ab). Meanwhile, Mary Magdalene and Mary the mother of Jesus observed where he had been laid (47).

Here, according to Schenke, we have the earliest account of the passion, the basis of the canonical Markan narrative, which has been embellished and completed with the addition of new historical and theological data. This primitive text seems to have originated with the Hellenistic Christians of Jerusalem led by Stephen (see Acts 6–7). The account, as noted above, is precisely an *account* of a Jesus who was the suffering messiah. The narrative conceals a polemic. Unable to accept the figure of a messiah who suffered, dying shamefully on a cross, the Jews had persecuted this group of his followers and had liquidated Stephen. Other exegetes prefer to assign the origin of the text to the mission to the pagans (Acts 8).

The other evangelists complete the pre-Markan and Markan texts with other data. The historicity of these data is the object of a considerable amount of discussion, but the precarious character of the fonts themselves excludes any hope of consensus. Furthermore, the evangelists seem not to have had the benefit of any eyewitnesses when it comes to Jesus' trial. What they are reporting is theological reflection, with a strong accent on Old Testament texts. Lohse's observation is to the point:

> This is why the early Christians could hardly speak of the suffering and death of Jesus without employing the language of the Old Testament. In the various episodes of the passion story Old Testament quotations and expressions are to be found at every point, not just where a scriptural quotation is expressly prefaced by a specific introduction but even more frequently as an integral part of the continuing narrative. And it is not merely a case of certain events in the *via dolorosa* being described in terms of Old Testament imagery, events such as the mockery of Jesus, his

crucifixion between two malefactors, and his burial. On the contrary, there is no doubt but that study of the Old Testament also led to the inclusion in the passion story of individual sayings from the Psalms and the Prophets in such a way that they helped to shape the narrative.

Frequently we can no longer determine with any assurance whether particular statements and expressions in the passion story are intended to recount actual happenings or whether they have simply been taken over as a part of the proof from Scripture and then used to embellish the narrative [Lohse, 9–10].

Thus for example the passage, "They tried to give him wine drugged with myrrh" (Mark 15:23, 36 and parallels), is an exact match for the text of Psalm 69:22. Then when we read that lots were cast for Jesus' garments (Mark 15:24 and par.), what we have is a perfect parallel with Psalm 22:19. Jesus' last, solemn outcry, *"Eloi, Eloi, lama sabachthani? . . . My God, my God, why have you forsaken me?"* (Mark 15:34), is a word-for-word citation of Psalm 22:2. The cry, however, is probably historical; the words are preserved in Hebrew, and not only in the Greek of the Gospel of Mark. But with the rest, we no longer know whether we are dealing with actual events, which later reminded the primitive community of things they had read in the Old Testament, or just the reverse; Old Testament texts suggesting the introduction of these vignettes into the passion accounts, thereby transforming the narrative from a literal historical account to an interpretive one.

JESUS' JOURNEY TO JERUSALEM

Before proceeding to an examination of Jesus' trial and sentencing, we may well ask why Jesus went to Jerusalem in the first place. Here he would be crucified, and here, according to the synoptic tradition, was the only occasion in his adult life that he ever visited the holy city.

Jesus thought of himself as a prophet. He expected the imminent irruption of the reign of God. His proclamation of that reign throughout Galilee enjoyed a certain popularity, it is true, but all in all it was not really very successful. The Gospels make it quite clear that Jesus' prophetical peregrinations were dogged by failure. Mark says right from the beginning (Mark 3:6) that Jesus will meet with opposition, and that the Pharisees will enter into a conspiracy with Herod's party in order to find a way to eliminate him. Then it will be the chief priests and the doctors of the law (Mark 11:18) who will oppose him. Jesus' lamentation over Chorazin, Capernaum, and Bethsaida (Quelle/Luke 10:13–15; Matt. 11:20–24) shows that his message was rejected. Gradually his isolation grows. According to John 6:67, the disciples abandon him. Now he is left alone with the twelve. But his failure neither impresses nor depresses him, for, like all the prophets who have preceded him, he is convinced of the truth of his proclamation.

Jesus' concrete motivation for deciding to go up to Jerusalem is beyond recovery today. Mark says only that the son of man had to go to Jerusalem to suffer and die. This triplicated "had to" (Mark 8:31; 9:31; 10:33), as we shall see more clearly below, denotes not absolute, fatalistic necessity, but the will of God, for Jesus' death will be his means of doing that will. Here we have a theological interpretation introjected into the text by the first Christians, who understood Christ's death as pertaining to God's dispensation in the plan of redemption. The evangelists favor us with no further clarification. In Luke 13:33 Jesus says that a prophet must die in Jerusalem, and these words echo something of the awareness on the part of the historical Jesus that he was the eschatological prophet. He expects the tragic death of any prophet. Jerusalem, for the Old Testament, was the theological place, the theological locus in the literal sense of the word, par excellence. It is in Jerusalem that all the great historico-salvific decrees of the divine plan must be verified. It is here that the mighty combat between the forces of good and evil, between the messiah and his enemies, will be waged. Steeped in such concepts himself, Jesus decides to make the trip to Jerusalem. There the last card will be played. There the reign of God will either burst forth in all its glory, or be stopped in its tracks.

ENTRY INTO JERUSALEM

The sacred writers' concern with the Old Testament text and with a theology of the suffering messiah is so overpowering in the account of Jesus' entry into Jerusalem as we have it today that the historical and the interpretive elements of the narrative can no longer be sorted out. Mark 11:1 says that Jesus comes up to Jerusalem from Jericho, by way of Bethany and Bethphage on the Mount of Olives, and approaches the city. The scene in which the disciples are sent in quest of the colt (Mark 11:3–8) is in correspondence with Genesis 49:11 and Zechariah 9:9, where we read that the messiah who is to deliver Jerusalem will come from the Mount of Olives seated on a beast of burden. The cries of Hosanna hark back to Psalm 118:25, and served the primitive church as a profession of faith in the messiah, not as a cry for help, in the original sense of the expression, but as an acclamation of faith. Lohse says:

> It is not Mark's intention at all to present here merely a historical report. His purpose is rather, even at the very beginning of his larger narrative of Jesus' last days and journey to the cross, to emphasize just who this Christ is who thus enters into suffering. The evangelist mentions "the kingdom of our father David that is coming" in order thereby to declare that in this Lord now walking toward the cross the whole of God's history with Israel finds its fulfillment and culmination [Lohse, 25].

The basic fact of Jesus' entry into Jerusalem is probably historical. It was common in Palestine to see a teacher riding on an animal, his disciples accompanying him on foot. And so Jesus and his followers enter Jerusalem— but not in great triumph, which would have been impossible in the presence of the Romans occupying the city. The entry was an ordinary, commonplace, little happening, taken in itself, but it was embellished after the resurrection. The community had begun to understand that the seeming banality of the event concealed a deeper meaning: the *Messiah* was entering *the City*. As John would say:

> At first, the disciples did not understand all this, but after Jesus was glorified they recalled that the people had done to him precisely what had been written about him [John 12:16].

Each of the evangelists paints his particular picture of Jesus entering Jerusalem, on the basis of a theological understanding after the event. It would be too lengthy to examine each portrait in detail. For Matthew, for example, Jesus' entry provoked stupefaction in the people, who kept referring to him as "the prophet Jesus from Nazareth in Galilee" (Matt. 21:11).

Then Jesus goes to the temple. He cleanses it. He heals the blind and lame, and receives the acclamations of the children (Matt. 21:14–17). God's servant carries and cures our sufferings, and is surrounded by the lowly and the despised, who represent his true community. This is the meaning Matthew attributes to the entry into Jerusalem. This is theology, then, rather than factual history.

PURIFICATION OF THE TEMPLE

Matthew and Mark, before recounting the purification of the temple, report the cursing of the sterile fig tree. The next day Peter reminds Jesus of the event. This scene is probably an extension of the parable of the sterile fig tree (Luke 13:6–9). Here the tree has the symbolic function of revealing the seriousness of the judgment looming over Jerusalem, in these days when the messiah is in the holy city.

There are good reasons for accepting the account of the purification of the temple as historical. The synoptics situate it during Jesus' last days (which is when it must have occurred historically), although John, for theological reasons, situates it at the beginning of Jesus' public life. The meaning of the account, as we shall see later, lies in its revelation of the historical Jesus' messianic consciousness, and in its focus on the question of his authority. With what right, power, authority, does he do this (Mark 11:28 and par.)? From this point forward, Jesus and the authorities are locked in deadly combat. Matters rapidly approach a crisis. The texts bring this into relief with their accounts of the disputes that ensue between Jesus and the Pharisees and Sadducees (Mark 11:27–12:40). Mark 13 contains the eschatological passages that tell of peril and terror hanging over the community. But the Son of Man will come in the capacity of a judge, and deliver his own. The purport of these texts is to reaffirm the notion that he who is presently opposed and persecuted by the authorities is the Son of Man and the eschatological judge. He will judge and punish his enemies. This is postpaschal reflection, then, and a rereading of the meaning of the painful journey of the messiah. The historical event is subsumed in a theological framework.

LAST SUPPER

The present form of the Last Supper accounts is fraught with critical problems. There is everything to indicate that they were introduced into the passion accounts from without. They seem to have developed independently, in Hellenistic circles, where Jewish customs were not known very precisely. We note this ignorance in Mark's introduction: "On the first day of Unleavened Bread, when it was customary to sacrifice the paschal lamb" (Mark 14:12). There is a contradiction here. The lamb was actually sacrificed the day before, on the eve of the feast of Unleavened Bread. The Hellenistic author is no longer very familiar with the customs of the Jews.

Then of course we also have the chronological discrepancy between the synoptics and John. In John the Last Supper is celebrated on Tuesday night. In the synoptics it is celebrated on Wednesday night. In John, Christ died on the eve of the day of the Jewish Passover, when the lambs were slain. In the synoptics, he died on the following day, on Friday.

Many theories have been advanced to explain this discrepancy. The solution seems to be that the respective chronologies are not historical but theological. Matthew, Mark, and Luke are concerned to accentuate the intimate theological connection of the Last Supper with the Jewish Passover. The new Lord's Supper has replaced the ancient repast. The celebration of the people's deliverance from Egypt is now the festival of the lord of definitive liberation. John's theological emphasis is different. Christ is our Passover, as the primitive church said (see 1 Cor. 5:7). He died on the day the paschal lamb was sacrificed, to demonstrate its replacement by a worthier victim. Jesus' death ushers in a new order. Away with the Old Testament feast—the feast of the Son of God who died and was raised is at hand! Both the synoptics and John wrote in view of the primitive preaching, and different kerygmatic approaches dictate different approaches to doctrine.

These theological interpretations, however, cannot conjure away the historical problem. Was Jesus' supper a Jewish Passover meal or was it not? It will not be easy to find the answer in the framework of the gospel accounts of the Lord's Supper as we have them today. In other words, we should not look for the answer in the gospel accounts of the passion, because there the Last Supper is reported in a theological, not a historical, framework.

One approach to a solution would be to examine the actual *formula* of words used at the Last Supper, which, as we know from 1 Corinthians 11, had already been handed down in independent form in the early communities. However, even the traditional words actually fail to afford a solid historical base, in spite of Paul's words, "The Lord Jesus on the night in which he was betrayed took bread" (1 Cor. 11:23). This is no demonstration that what Paul is about to report necessarily took place in connection with the Jewish Passover meal; as we have seen in Saint John, it could have occurred on the day before. As we know, Jesus took many meals with his disciples, as well as with tax collectors and Pharisees, eating bread and drinking wine to the point of being called a glutton and a drunkard (Matt. 11:19 and par.). The Last Supper, then, could have been the Passover meal, or it could have been an ordinary meal—the final one, the farewell meal, this time—taken by Jesus with his own.

On the other hand, the *content* of the words of the eucharistic supper have no connection with the words pronounced at the Jewish Passover meal. In the latter, an explanation is given of the bitter herbs and unleavened bread. The herbs were bitter, to symbolize the bitter life led by the Jews under the Egyptians, and the bread was unleavened because, in the haste of their flight to freedom, the Israelites had been able to take with them only bread that had not yet been leavened. At Jesus' meal there is no mention of either herbs or dough. We hear only of bread and wine. Jesus' words are pronounced not within a liturgical action, as in the Jewish meal, but at the distribution of the bread and wine.

As for the actual words used by Jesus, we do not know their exact historical formulation. We have them by way of two traditions, (1) that of Mark and Matthew, and (2) that of Luke and Paul. According to most exegetes, including Schürmann, Hahn, Conzelmann, Kümmel, and others, Jesus' exact historical formulation can no longer be reconstructed.

Nevertheless, we must not overlook one crucial datum. The important thing in the Last Supper is not the precise formulation of Jesus' words, but the meal itself, the whole action. Within this action, the purpose of the words is to bring out a latent meaning inherent in the action. The words are inserted here in view of the action as a whole. The supper is the Lord's farewell meal. Something final and definitive is about to occur between Jesus and his own. The meal means good-bye. And the bread and wine do have their Passover context. In the Jewish feast, the father of the family takes bread into his hands and blesses it. All answer, "Amen." At the end of the meal he does the same with the wine, whereupon all at table help themselves to the bread and wine. Christ must have celebrated this ritual, conferring upon it a definitive meaning.

Despite the literary differences between the two traditions of the Last Supper account, they share two common elements: the notion of the covenant, and the notion of a sacrificial self-surrender. Accordingly, we have an eschatological theme (that of the covenant) and a soteriological theme (the surrender of a body and the shedding of blood). The eschatological theme, as we shall see below, is altogether consonant with Jesus' historical act. The other, the sacrificial theme, which we shall have to consider as well, is difficult to attribute to Jesus. Meanwhile, the basic meaning of the act of Jesus' distributing bread and wine to the company at table is clear. It is a symbol of the imminent irruption of the reign of God. Jesus had compared that reign to a meal on several occasions during his lifetime (Matt. 8:11; Luke 14:15–24; Mark 2:18–22; etc.). The treatments in Luke 22:15–18 and parallels, and Mark 14:25, preserve this eschatological content of the Last Supper very well. The reign of God is about to dawn, the eschatological meal is about to be served. The Last Supper is an authentic indication of Jesus' eschatological mentality.

After the resurrection, when the meaning of Jesus' death as sacrifice and free self-surrender became clear, a new meaning was bestowed on the bread and wine, expressing this sacrificial attitude on Jesus' part. This meaning, however, is layered over the other, primitive meaning, the eschatological sense of the symbol, and the community was always careful to preserve the eschatological sense as well, as we may gather from Paul's testimony: "Every time, then, you eat this bread and drink this cup, you proclaim the death of the Lord *until he comes!*" And we know that the first Christians concluded their eucharistic gatherings with the eschatological cry, "Maranatha, come, Lord Jesus!"

Finally, we might ask: What is the connection between the eucharist, instituted by Jesus as a sacrament, and the Last Supper?

The institution of the eucharist must be understood in the context of the whole mystery of Jesus Christ. It cannot be reduced to the words and deeds of Jesus of Nazareth during the time he lived and walked in Palestine. His activity extends beyond his death, into the age of the church. The whole apostolic period is a constitutive time of the church, and hence of the definitive, official Christian revelation. The eucharist as a sacrament springs from the totality of the Christ event: from the activity of Jesus of Nazareth, of course, who shared a last meal with his intimates, at which he did certain things and pronounced certain words—whose meaning, at the time, was limited to an eschatological one—but then, too, from the activity of the Jesus who was raised, and who acted in conjunction with his Spirit to move the apostles to celebrate the Lord's Supper time and again, repeating his words and gestures in a sacrificial, ecclesiological sense and in a new context—that of the continuity of the history and mission of a church charged with carrying the message of the resurrection to the ends of the earth. All these elements, these stages, with their distinct mediations, constitute the work of Jesus Christ, for without him we should be unable adequately to understand them in the manner in which we understand Jesus' work, historically, today.

But returning now to our own reflection, which is concerned strictly with the historical Jesus, we ask: What motivated the inclusion of our present eucharistic narrative, which developed in another context, in the passion account?

All indications are that the motive was theological. The passion is the story of our redemption, accomplished through the sacrifice of the messiah, the suffering just one. The eucharistic texts had already developed this sacrificial theology. Nothing was more obvious, therefore, than that they should be inserted into the passion accounts. Their development may have been independent, but their theological contexts are the same.

TEMPTATION IN GETHSEMANI

The synoptics tell of Jesus' agony in the Garden of Olives moments before his arrest—his anguish, his desperate prayer, and even, according to Luke

22:44, his perspiration, resembling great drops of blood. The account as we have it is shot through with theology, in response to the needs of the primitive community for guidance and examples.

Again, then, Jesus is tempted. He is subjected to a terrible trial: "My heart is filled with sorrow to the point of death" (Mark 14:34). "*Abba* (O Father), you have the power to do all things. Take this cup away from me" (Mark 14:36). What is this test, this temptation?

Most probably it is the great trial that signals the irruption of the reign of God, the tribulation of which the apocalyptical texts speak in fear and trembling. It would not be fear in the face of death, then, but a more fundamental terror still: the great eschatological peril in which the children of light, the followers of the Messiah, will be placed by the children of darkness. This is the "hour," the culminating moment in which everything is to be decided. Well does Mark say that Jesus "fell to the ground, praying that if it were possible this hour might pass him by" (Mark 14:35).

The wording of Jesus' prayer seems to have been composed by the primitive Christian community. The texts themselves make it clear that there was no one to hear what Jesus said. All were sleeping. But early christology interpreted Jesus' whole historical journey in the light of passages from the Old Testament, because this would render intelligible the mystery of his humiliation and glorification. The scene before us is no exception. Jesus' messianic temptation and the prayer rising up from this great existential trial were understood in light of those prayers par excellence, the Psalms, and interpreted in words taken from the Psalms. The Psalms are full of the prayer of the suffering just man, the one subjected to trial and crying out to God, who hears and comforts him. In this perspective, the words of the Letter to the Hebrews, which hands down this tradition of a tested, praying Jesus, become perfectly intelligible:

> In the days when he was in the flesh, he offered prayers and supplications with loud cries and tears to God, who was able to save him from death, and he was heard because of his reverence [Heb. 5:7].

Jesus' admonition, "Be on guard and pray that you may not be put to the test. The spirit is willing but nature is weak" (Mark 14:38), is very probably an instructive logion composed by the first communities, but it suits Jesus' situation and disposition remarkably. "Nature" (literally, "flesh") and "spirit" here must not be understood in the Pauline sense of "flesh" and "spirit," but in the sense in which they were used by the Judaism of the time of Christ, a sense well attested by the texts of the Qumran community. According to the Qumran documents, the spirit of truth and the spirit of falsehood are locked in a combat so fierce that the very human heart, and the children of light themselves, become its battleground. How can we prevail, we who feel the weakness of our "flesh," our fragility, so keenly, if the struggle is being waged within our very hearts? Our only hope will lie in suppliant, fervent prayer. But the moment of this final combat must come, for it will eventuate in the victory of God, precisely at the moment ("hour") when the temptation, the trial, reaches its paroxysm. Saint John, too, espouses this tradition, when, outside the context of the passion, he has Christ say:

> My soul is troubled now,
> yet what should I say—
> Father, save me from this hour?
> But it was for this that I came to this hour
>   [John 12:27].

The primitive Christian awareness of a last great trial for Jesus, and his mighty, victorious effort, in prayer, to bear up under that trial, led the community to compose the scene in the Garden of Gethsemani. Its contents, then, are not restricted to historical fact, but emerge from a christological reflection on Jesus: Jesus was tempted, but he overcame the temptation, and let this be an example to the community. The scene in Gethsemani possesses a matchless precedential value. It gives us a marvelous picture of Jesus' profound humanness, and at the same time it represents his complete openness to God in the midst of danger.

TRIAL AND SENTENCING

A military detail arrives in the garden. Judas leads the soldiers to Jesus. Jesus is arrested. Now the judicial portion of the action against him is under way. The accounts as we have them are somewhat divergent. Mark, the oldest, is rather summary. Matthew and Luke expand Mark considerably. John follows his own devices.

I shall not enter into a detailed discussion of the points of agreement and disagreement among the four canonical accounts. Exegetes are fairly unanimous that there is little historical certainty with regard to what occurred in Jesus' official interrogations at the hands of the religious and civil authorities. Nor can we determine precisely the dates of his arrest, sentencing, and crucifixion: the first Christians were unconcerned to transmit to us a precise chronology of events. But they were concerned about transmitting to us their faith that the suffering just one who undergoes these tribulations is the awaited of nations, the messiah, the savior of the world.

Historically certain are the fact of the crucifixion, the sentencing at the hands of Pilate, and the inscription over Jesus' head in the three languages familiar to the Jews. The other elements of our accounts are either theology, or at least a theologization of the facts, composed by the community in the light of the resurrection, and upon reflection on the Old Testament.

I shall follow the scenario composed from a study of the four evangelists by the great Catholic scholar Josef Blinzler, who bases his work on historical criticism, and is well aware of the limitations that that criticism imposes on our certitude of the various elements in our composite picture. I note, however, that Blinzler's synopsis enjoys considerable support among other scholars.

There were two trials, a religious one under the auspices of the Jewish authorities, and a political one conducted by the representative of the Roman occupation forces, Pontius Pilate.

The Religious Trial: Jesus Sentenced for Blasphemy

Taken into custody in the Garden of Olives, Jesus is brought to the palace of the high priest, Caiphas, there to spend the night. The trial itself cannot get under way at once, because the 71-member Sanhedrin was prohibited by law from meeting at that hour of the night. But former high priest Annas, father-in-law of Caiphas, and other religious leaders take advantage of the interval to interrogate Jesus concerning his doctrine, his disciples, and his intentions. Long and extensively have the exegetes debated whether this interrogation was an official one or not. Be this as it may, at all events Jesus refuses to give any answers. The synoptics tell of Jesus' ridicule and torture, phenomena familiar enough in the underworld of the henchmen of the organs of repression.

The following day, in the southeast corner of the temple, the Sanhedrin meets in council (*boule* or *lishkathha gazith*—see Luke 22:66), with high priest Caiphas as official inquisitor. The session opens with the taking of depositions. Historically the content of this testimony remains rather unclear. It probably dealt with Jesus' liberal position with respect to the Sabbath (Mark 2:23–28 and par.; John 5:9–18)—that ongoing scandal in Jewish eyes and the mark of a seducer or false prophet (Matt. 27:63; John 7:12; Luke 23:2, 5, 14)—and his reputed expulsion of demons in the name of demons (Mark 3:22; Matt. 9:34). The witnesses, however, contradict one another (Mark 14:56). Another most grave allegation, lodged in bygone times against Jeremiah (Jer. 26:1–19) and costing him his life, is thrown up to Jesus as well: the story that he has claimed to be able to destroy the temple and rebuild it in three days (Mark 14:58; John 2:19). But here as elsewhere, the testimony is conflicting.

Enter Caiphas—who, after subjecting Jesus to close questioning, declares that the defendant deserves the death penalty for the crime of blasphemy (Mark 14:64). What blasphemy has Jesus committed? According to Mark 14:61–62, it is somehow in his answer to the high priest's question, "Are you the Messiah, the Son of the Blessed One?" Jesus answers, "I am; and you will see the Son of Man seated at the right hand of the Power and coming with the clouds of heaven." Catholic and Protestant exegetes alike have long wrestled with the problem of whether we are dealing with historical material here, or with a profession of faith in which the primitive community, in the light of the resurrection and the Old Testament, has identified Jesus with the messiah-christ and the son of man of Daniel 7. It is difficult to answer this question by purely exegetical methods. We must admit that the gospels have no intention of being "history" in the modern sense of the word. Their intent is kerygmatic. They are a profession of faith. History and the interpretation of history, under the light of faith, blend together into a vital unity.

Meanwhile, we may observe that to declare oneself the messiah-christ did not of itself constitute blasphemy. Various liberators had presented themselves as the messiah before Jesus of Nazareth, yet none of them had ever been sentenced to death for doing so.

In the second place, we notice that the title "messiah-christ" is here joined to another one, "Son of the Blessed One"—"Blessed One" being a circumlocution for the name of God. The expression "son of God" was a familiar one in the Hellenistic world. In Judaism, however, despite Psalm 2:7, which speaks of the messiah-christ (the "anointed") as God's "son" ("this day I have begotten you"), was not applied to the messiah in a physical sense, but only in the sense of the familiar figure in which oriental royalty were referred to as the offspring of God. Judaism, unlike paganism, rejected the notion of a king's divine filiation. The messiah was not called by the title "son of God." It was the primitive Christian community that would be responsible for this, applying to a Christ raised from the dead all the titles of grandeur they knew, whether Jewish, Hellenistic, or Judeo-Hellenistic. The high priest, then, should not have couched his question in these terms.

Other exegetes find the "blasphemy" in terms of Deuteronomy 17:12: "Any man who has the insolence to refuse to listen to the priest who officiates there in the ministry of the Lord, your God, or to the judge, shall die." This determination was applied precisely in the condemnation of false prophets or false teachers, as we know from the history of Judaism after A.D. 70. In this hypothesis, Jesus' silence in the presence of the supreme judicial authority of the nation constituted a contempt of court tantamount to blasphemy, so that the death penalty could be invoked (Bowker's thesis, adopted by Schillebeeckx, *Jesus,* 277–82).

The argumentation for this hypothesis is not very convincing. The historical testimonials postdate A.D. 70. Besides, Jesus' accusation as a false prophet does not stand out very strikingly among the other allegations.

What we can say with certainty is that, in the last moments of his life, Jesus had a clear, precise awareness of his mission and of the link between his own person and the reign of God. Human destiny, the fate of the world in the sight of God, lay with him. Probably this awareness dawned in all its clarity during Caiphas's solemn interrogation.

A claim like this is a claim to some manner of divine role. And this for a faithful Jew was as blasphemous as extreme monophysitism would be for a Christian. Add to this the measureless scandal of the contrast between a like arrogation of the sphere of the divine, and the claimant's seeming weakness— the inadequacy of his means for the mission he says is his, and his present condition, that of a helpless victim at the mercy of torturers. Does such a personage incarnate Yahweh's promises of the people's total liberation, especially their deliverance from political enemies? Surely this is blasphemy, and the voice vote of the 71-member Sanhedrin is unanimous: "They answered, 'He deserves death!' " (Matt. 26:66).

One would think that the Sanhedrin could have sentenced Jesus to death by stoning. But apparently, although this is still an open question, the right to pronounce a capital sentence was reserved to the Romans, so that the domestic religious authority was deprived of this right, as we read in the Talmud (well substantiated in this instance). The stoning of Stephen (Acts 7:54–8:3) and the beheading of James (Acts 12:2) the brother of John—the sons of Zebedee—seem to constitute, respectively, an act of mob violence and an overextension of authority on the part of Herod. Saint John's "We may not put anyone to death" (John 18:31) enjoys historical support.

The Political Trial: Jesus Condemned as a Guerrilla Subversive

The Sanhedrin's decision must be ratified by the political judiciary, and so a second trial is held. This time the presiding judge is the Roman procurator, Pilate. Jesus' adversaries employ a clever tactic, transforming the religious indictment into a political one. Only thus will they have any hope of having their allegations heard and of seeing Jesus condemned to be executed. They accuse him of seeking to place himself at the head of a political liberation movement (that of the messiah to come), indeed of claiming to be the king of the Jews (Mark 15:26 and par.), and of seeking to subvert the entire country in order to bring his ambitions to realization (Luke 23:2, 5, 14). According to the pre-Markan account, to Pilate's question whether he was the king of the Jews (Mark 15:2), Jesus did not respond, maintaining a silence of solemn and sovereign dignity. If Jesus had admitted the charge, as he does in the present version of the Gospels, which had developed a theology of the defendant as the *Kyrios*—lord of the cosmos and king of the Jews and the universe—who had been raised from the dead, Pilate's reaction, thrice expressed in the passion narrative (Luke 23:4, 15, 22), "I do not find a case against this man," would be unintelligible. Probably Pilate came to grasp in the course of his questioning that he was not dealing with a political revolutionary on the pattern of the Zealots, who sought the violent overthrow of the Roman occupation:

> Saint Mark is among those who employ the expression "king" because this term has a close connection with "reign," the key word of Jesus' preaching. The literary device is an intelligent one, and seeks to show Jesus as a different kind of king: a king of ridicule (Mark 15:18, 32), a monarch enjoying worse repute than the insurrectionist who is released in his stead (15:9–12), a king publicly sentenced (15:2, 4) and crucified naked (15:26–27) [K. Rahner, "Mittler"].

As a way out of the impasse, Pilate returns Jesus to Herod, who is sojourning in Jerusalem at the moment (Luke 23:6–12). Herod was tetrarch of Galilee, the principal region of Jesus' activity. Now he can speak his piece, and Jesus is interrogated by him as well. Jesus' silence offends the tetrarch, who returns him, clad in a parody of royal vesture, to Pilate. This scene, presented only by Luke, is apparently of legendary origin, and Martin Dibelius has shown this very well (*Botschaft,* 278–92). It is probably a midrashic historicization of Psalm 2:1: "The kings of the earth rise up, and the princes conspire together against the Lord and against his anointed"—that is, against "his Christ."

The Barabbas episode, too, would seem to be legendary. There is no evidence in any other document of a custom whereby the populace, once a year, would ask that a prisoner be freed. The episodes involving Herod and Barabbas, the *Ecce Homo,* and the scene of Pilate's washing his hands seem to be at the service of the apologetic motif of the primitive church. The point is that Christianity does not represent a danger to the Roman state. Pilate has comported himself as an honorable Roman citizen. Christians have nothing against the empire and its representatives. This purpose of this apologetic motif, in turn, is to facilitate the preaching of the gospel in the imperial atmosphere. Hence the tendency to exculpate Pilate and place practically the whole blame on the Jews and the leaders who manipulated them. This concern of the Gospels is more explicit later on. Thus the apocryphal Gospel of Peter has Herod pronounce the death sentence on Jesus and command its execution; Pilate washes his hands in token of his innocence, but the Jews and Herod refuse to do so, thus assuming total responsibility in the matter. Indeed, the process of Pilate's exculpation will reach the point that Tertullian will consider him a crypto-Christian (*Apologeticum,* 21, 24). Another tradition will hold that Pilate eventually suffered martyrdom for the sake of Christ. The Ethiopian Church still honors him, along with Judas, as a saint.

Roman sources, meanwhile, paint a picture of Pilate, who had become procurator in A.D. 26, as an individual of extreme "venality, plunder, ill behavior, crime, one summary execution after another, and mindless cruelty" (Philo, *Leg. ad Caium,* 38). Ten years later he was removed from office, on the occasion of bloody massacres among the Samaritans. Along with the Roman legate in Syria, he was indicted, discharged, and expelled from Palestine. This image of Pilate is difficult to reconcile with the one in the gospels, and so we are inclined to suppose an apologetic concern on the part of the latter.

Only under threat of seeming to be Caesar's enemy (John 19:21) does Pilate yield to the cries of the populace and their leaders. Mark says simply: "After he had had Jesus scourged, he handed him over to be crucified" (Mark 15:15). And he records the *titulus,* in three languages: *Iesus Nazarenus Rex Iudaeorum.*

The Gospels assign the main burden of guilt for Jesus' condemnation to "the Jews," whose leaders (the "chief priests") see in Jesus' popularity a dangerous threat to their positions of power and prestige. The Sadducees, masters of the marketplace, whether in the temple or elsewhere in Jerusalem, and enjoying a great deal of influence with the Sanhedrin, are afraid that Jesus' activity could provoke a reaction on the part of the Romans, in which case they too would be threatened in their position. The Pharisees loathe Jesus, for his liberal attitude toward the law and toward the God of the sacred traditions: Jesus has been perverting the people, they feel. Political, national, and religious considerations, then, all conspire to call for the prophet's liquidation. The Jerusalemites, incited by their threatened, fearful leaders, exert pressure on Pilate, who, out of cowardice, and fear of loss of favor with Caesar, orders Jesus to be tortured to death.

Jesus' death was judicial murder, then—*Justizmord* (Blinzler, 243), and not some kind of judicial error. Far from being a mistake of any kind, it was the fruit of malevolent interest, and evil will. Were we to wish to define the crime more precisely, we might say it was a religio-political murder via an abuse of justice. The New Testament never speaks of deicide (but see 2 Thess. 2:15).

CRUCIFIXION

Now that the capital sentence has been pronounced, Jesus is handed over to the torture process. The Roman legionaries would subject to horrible torments the poor wretches who were sentenced to death. They would strip them naked, scourge them, and subject them to the most unmentionable indignities and debasing ridicule, quite after the manner of the inhumane, albeit common, procedures used with alleged political subversives in our own day.

Mark says, laconically: "When they had finished mocking him, they stripped him of the purple, dressed him in his own clothes, and led him out to crucify him" (Mark 15:20).

The method of torture known as crucifixion, "that most barbarous and horrible chastisement" (Cicero, *Against Verres,* book 2, 5, 65, 165), was reserved all but exclusively for political rebels and slaves. After preliminary torture, the condemned were obliged to carry their own instruments of execution to the place of capital punishment. Arriving there, they were stripped, nailed to the crossed stakes, and raised some two or three meters above the ground. We know that victims might agonize for days before finally expiring. Jesus died after only three hours, hanging on the cross from midday until three o'clock in the afternoon (Mark 15:33).

Mark recounts that Simon of Cyrene helped Jesus to carry his cross, and names Simon's sons, Alexander and Rufus, names probably known in the Markan community (Luke omits the names). It would surely be understandable that after three torture sessions (the one the night before, a second in Caiphas's palace, and a third in connection with Annas's questioning as reported in Luke 22:63–65), and after the trials held by the Sanhedrin (Mark 14:65) and before Pilate (Mark 15:15–20), Jesus would have been extremely weakened. The encounters with Mary, his mother, and with Veronica, on the other hand, would appear to be legendary. From the fourth century onward we hear of a Veronica, identified in the West with Martha and in the East with a certain "Berenice" (an alternative form of "Veronica"). According to legend, it is she who went to Tiberius Caesar to denounce Pilate, obtaining the latter's discharge and sentencing. Then she had a portrait of Jesus painted and showed it to Tiberius, who was converted by it. Another version recounts that she met Jesus on his way to the Place of the Skull, wiped his face with her veil, and received on her veil, in recompense, the imprint of the suffering countenance of her Lord.

The meeting with the "daughters of Jerusalem" (Luke 23:27) would seem to be historical. We know from historical sources (in the Talmud) that women customarily administered an aromatic wine to the condemned in order to relieve his sufferings. The words Jesus addresses them, however, are all from the Old Testament, and are Luke's way of expressing what Jesus must have said to them.

The two brigands had probably been sentenced as Zealots for a guerrilla attack on the Romans. Luke 23:37 recalls Isaiah 53:12: "He was counted among the wicked." The taunts at the foot of the cross are inspired by Old Testament passages, especially by the Psalms, and have the purpose of emphasizing the patience with which the suffering just one bears up under all his trials. Luke 23:40-43 enriches the text with part of a legend about one of the brigands, having Jesus say to him: "I assure you: this day you will be with me in paradise" (Luke 23:43).

Jesus' last cry, *"Eloi, Eloi, lama sabachthani?"* (Mark 15:34), is crucial for an understanding of Jesus' awareness of himself and his mission. Here, in my opinion, we have the key to Jesus' historical life. The other six "words of Christ" (Luke 23:34, 43, 46; John 19:26, 28, 30) are of doubtful historicity.

The "signs" that ensue upon Jesus' death are further literary devices for the purpose of emphasizing its meaning and importance. Thus, for example, Mark 15:33 and parallels, which speak of a darkness over the whole earth from the sixth to the ninth hour, are a rehearsal of the familiar apocalyptical figure (see Mark 13:24 and par.) representing the end of the present age, which, according to the Gospels, comes with the death of Jesus Christ.

The Gospels likewise speak of the sundering of the temple veil, from top to bottom (Mark 15:38 and par.). This is not a historical occurrence, but a literary code for the inauguration, with the death of Jesus, of our direct access to God (Heb. 10:19-20).

Matthew 27:52-53 reports, further: "The earth quaked, boulders split, tombs opened. Many bodies of saints who had fallen asleep were raised. After Jesus' resurrection they came forth from their tombs and entered the holy city and appeared to many." This too is a literary device, representing a realized eschatology: with Jesus, the end of the world has come. The end of the world, in the apocalyptical understanding, would entail the resurrection of the dead, along with certain cosmic signs. Jesus is the first of those raised up, and therefore, with his death, the old world has ended and the new one has begun.

An ancient formula of the Christian kerygma proclaimed: "Christ died for our sins in accordance with the Scriptures; . . . he was buried" (1 Cor. 15:3-4). Early Christians were concerned to emphasize that Jesus had really died. The Gospels recount that he was honorably buried, not by his relatives, but by civil officials (Acts 13:29). The law explicitly prohibited leaving the dead bodies of the crucified on their crosses overnight (Deut. 21:23), even apart from the fact that the following day was the Sabbath.

Mark concludes his account of the passion with the centurion's profession of faith: "Clearly this man was the Son of God!" (Mark 15:39). This is the profession of faith of the evangelist and his community, and serves as a challenge to anyone hearing his account: Can you not see in this tortured, crucified one the Son of God? Mark is writing in Rome, and thus places his mighty profession of faith in the mouth of a Roman officer, thereby inviting all Romans to come and follow after Jesus Christ.

Chapter 4

How Did Jesus Interpret His Death?

Now that we have considered Jesus' trial, sentencing, and crucifixion as a consequence of his life and of the praxis that he inaugurated, the question arises: Did Jesus anticipate his condemnation and violent death? Someone who makes the demands Jesus made, someone who questions the law and the meaning of the temple worship in view of a deeper truth, someone who arouses the enthusiasm of the masses through a proclamation charged with ideological concepts like the "reign of God" and "violence," must have reckoned with a reaction on the part of the watchdogs of the status quo: the Pharisees, champions of the law; the Sadducees, with their temple worship; and the Romans, political rulers of an occupied country. This is our first question, then, the question that arises most spontaneously in view of all the facts.

Secondly, however, there is another, and a more fundamental, question: How did Jesus interpret his own death? As a redemptive death? As a death by substitution? As the death of a martyred prophet?

Let me attempt to answer these two questions separately.

JESUS' ATTITUDE TOWARD THE PROSPECT OF A VIOLENT DEATH

The gospel texts insist that Jesus did not naively blunder his way to his death. He accepted his death. He took it upon himself freely. When finally arrested, he forbade the apostles to defend him (Matt. 26:52–56)—otherwise "How would the Scriptures be fulfilled?" (v. 56). In the Johannine version of the temptation in Gethsemani, he explicitly accepts the "cup" of his suffering (John 18:1–11).

The texts are clear, then, as to Jesus' willingness to die. But at the same time we have to admit that he did not go out of his way to be killed. His death was forced upon him. He had gotten into a set of circumstances from which there was no other honorable way out—no other solution that would not mean a

44

betrayal of his mission. His death was the "logical" outcome of a life like his, a life of such forthright condemnation of the religion and politics he saw around him. He did not seek his death, or wish for such a death. He was forced to accept it. He accepted it, however, not in a spirit of helpless resignation, or sovereign stoicism, but in human liberty, and hence as a person who rose above the exigencies of brute necessity. Jesus does not allow his life to be taken from him. He gives it up freely, as he has given himself all through his life.

But what Jesus was actively seeking was not death, but the proclamation and realization of the reign of God, and of the liberation that that reign would mean for human beings in terms of conversion and the acceptance of a Father of infinite goodness. For this message, along with the praxis it entailed, Jesus was ready to sacrifice all, including his very life. If the truth he preaches, testifies to, and lives, demand his death, he will accept death. Not that he seeks death for its own sake. But if death comes to him in consequence of his loyalty and fidelity—which in Jesus are stronger than death—then he will accept it. A death like that is a worthy one. A death like that was and is endured and lived— yes, lived—by any martyr prophet, yesterday as today.

Jesus knows the fate of the prophets (Matt 23:37; Luke 13:33–34; Acts 2:23). He is thought to be the Baptist, come back to life after his beheading (Mark 6:14). There were various plans or attempts to arrest him (Mark 11:18; John 7:30, 32, 44–52; 10:39) and to stone him (John 8:59; 10:31), and there was serious thought of having him eliminated (Mark 3:6; John 5:18; 11:49–50). This could not have all gone unnoticed by Jesus. Jesus was not naive. Besides, the incident of the violent expulsion of the hawkers and peddlers from the temple (Mark 11:15–16 and par.), and his remark, very probably his own, about the destruction of the temple (Mark 14:58 and par.), placed him in immediate danger of judicial proceedings at the hands of the religious authorities. Add to this the suspicion that he was harboring, among the twelve, individuals committed to violence and political subversion, as "Simon called the Zealot" (Luke 6:15 and par.; Acts 1:13), Judas the Iscariot (a nickname for a knife-wielder or murderer—that is, a Zealot), and the "Boanerges," or Sons of Thunder (Mark 3:17—a name reminiscent of the Zealot movements), and you have all the ingredients for very serious religious and political risk.

In the midst of it all, Jesus kept his complete trust in God. "Whoever tries to preserve his life will lose it; whoever loses it will keep it" (Luke 17:33 and par.; cf. 14:26; Mark 8:35).

And so we ask: Did Jesus expect a violent death? As we have seen, this is a legitimate question to ask, against the backdrop of his proclamation of the reign of God and its imminence. At the same time, however, Jesus obviously regards himself both as the eschatological prophet, and as the one who actualizes the new order that God shall momentarily introduce. Jesus *is* the reign of God, already present in our midst. Membership in the new order depends on adherence to his person. And what does this new order, this reign of God, entail? It means a new heaven and a new earth—transcendence of the fragility of this world and the banishment of all limits on life. But this implies victory over death. This being the case, could Jesus have expected to die on a cross?

Exegetico-theological Problems

The texts of the Gospels as we have them assert that Jesus knew what his last end would be. Indeed he had foretold it: he had said that he would be giving himself up for the redemption of "the many" (Mark 10:45)—that is, for all. The Gospels have Jesus utter three of these prophecies of his own death:

> He began to teach them that the Son of Man had to suffer much, be rejected by the elders, the chief priests, and the scribes, be put to death, and rise three days later [Mark 8:31].
> He was teaching his disciples in this vein: "The Son of Man is going to be delivered into the hands of men who will put him to death; three days after his death he will rise" [Mark 9:31].
> He began to tell them what was going to happen to him. "We are on our way up to Jerusalem, where the son of Man will be handed over to the chief priests and the scribes. They will condemn him to death and hand him over to the Gentiles, who will mock him and spit at him, flog him, and finally kill him. But three days later he will rise" [Mark 10:33].

Catholic and Protestant exegesis alike has debated the historical authenticity of such passages for many years now. The great majority of the exegetes, even those (such as Joachim Jeremias) who consider their content authentic, regard their formulation as nonhistorical. They bear all the marks of later work: they presuppose a detailed knowledge of Jesus' trial and of the whole Easter event.

All three passages, especially the third, present a thumbnail sketch of the passion. If these words, instead of being couched in the future tense, were in the past, we would recognize them as an account of Jesus' last days written by the primitive community. He went to Jerusalem, was handed over to the high priests and scribes, who sentenced him to death and then delivered him up to the pagans (the Romans), he was mocked, spat upon, scourged, put to death, and raised three days later.

And so, according to a goodly number of exegetes, these passages represent the primitive Christian preaching, not the words of the historical Jesus. For example, each prophecy opens with the expression "Son of Man." This is the personage who, according to the apocalyptic of the time, would come at the end of the ages on clouds of glory to judge and deliver the just. The Son of Man is never presented in a context of suffering, condemnation, and death.

But might not Jesus first have taken this title, and then, as he became aware of his approaching death, endowed it with fresh content? No, this hypothesis does not bear up under examination. Jesus uses the expression in the meaning it has in current apocalyptic: the Son of Man will come in his glory with his angels (Mark 8:38). His hearers would see the Son of Man coming on the clouds with great power and glory (Mark 13:26 and par.). The use of the expression "Son of Man," referring to Daniel 7, and the notion of this personage coming on the clouds of his majesty, are, to be sure, part of the oldest synoptic material. However, the identification of this Son of Man with the one condemned, killed, and raised is a theological elaboration of the primitive church. The prophecies, then, are what are called *vaticinia ex eventu*—"prophecies" after the fact, projections back into the time of Jesus' earthly life of things grasped after that earthly life, and with a clear theological import—namely, that everything that Jesus did or said before his death and resurrection is bound up with his destiny of death and resurrection, in a profound, indissoluble oneness. Jesus' death and resurrection, the primitive church is telling us, cannot be recounted without including an account of his life. The former is a consequence of the latter. The two elements taken in conjunction form the concrete, historical path that Jesus trod.

Another purpose of the prophecies is to reflect the consistency of God's plan. God did not abandon Jesus on Good Friday, as everything had seemed to indicate. No, God was with him still. Jesus was only implementing the secret, mysterious plan of God, carrying it out despite human activity and its wickedness. Jesus' death and resurrection are the work of God, for it is God who has guided all—without, of course, dispensing human beings from their responsibility, and this is why human beings are denounced in the prophecies. And so we read that the "Son of Man *had* to suffer much," *had* to die—this is apocalyptical, not Old Testament, language, used to express the sovereignty of God's plan, which unfolds irresistibly despite all efforts of human beings to block it. And of course there is also a note of consolation in this "had to." This paradoxical, painful divine necessity is subordinate to ultimate glory and fulfillment. In reference to Jesus, it means that death has yielded to resurrection.

Finally, there is the ever-present notion in the passion accounts that Jesus is the suffering just one. The Old Testament had proposed the notion of a suffering, but just, person who is rewarded and raised to glory. And so Jesus' mortal destiny was interpreted in that sense.

Evidence for Jesus' Gradual Awareness of His Coming End

The gospel texts afford us a number of indications that Jesus was only progressively aware of his last end.

1. The first seems to be the synoptic passage of the bridegroom who "will be taken away" (Mark 2:20 and par.). The context is polemical:

People came to Jesus with the objection, "Why do John's disciples and those of the Pharisees fast while yours do not?" Jesus replied: "How can the guests at a wedding fast as long as the groom is still among them? So long as the groom stays with them, they cannot fast. The day will come, however, when the groom will be taken away from them; on that day they will fast" [Mark 2:19–20].

This logion, however, according to numerous critics, is authentic only in part: "How can the guests at a wedding fast as long as the groom is still among them?" (Mark 2:19a). The second part would then be an addition made by the community, which, with its christological reflection now well under way, identified Jesus as the "bridegroom," an Old Testament figure for Yahweh, now used to justify the ascetical and penitential practices of a primitive Christian community that no longer availed itself of Jesus' liberties with respect to the law (see Taylor, 208–12; Percy, 233, 236).

2. Another passage to be considered here is in Luke 13. The Pharisees appear on the scene, and inform Jesus that Herod is seeking to put him to death. Jesus replies:

Go tell that fox, "Today and tomorrow I cast out devils and perform cures, and on the third day my purpose is accomplished. For all that, I must proceed on course today, tomorrow, and the day after, since no prophet can be allowed to die anywhere except in Jerusalem" [Luke 13:32–33].

This episode is considered to be basically historical. Verse 33, however, referring to death in Jerusalem, is considered by the great majority of exegetes, even the most conservative, to be incontestably the work of the Lukan redaction (Dupont, 299: "It is hightly unlikely that we are not dealing with an expansion by the evangelist"; see also George, 37).

This text, then, cannot be adduced as evidence that Jesus knew beforehand what manner of death he was to die.

3. Then come the familiar, and much-discussed, words of Mark 10:45: "The Son of Man has not come to be served but to serve—to give his life in ransom for the many"—that is, for everyone.

But we notice that this passage links the concept of "Son of Man" to the idea of his death—an association completely foreign to Judaism. Furthermore, exegesis has shown that the theme of *diakonia* ("service") had its proper *Sitz im Leben*, its vital context, in the meal of tradition of Christians in the primitive church. Several times Jesus employs the figure of serving at table at the feast of the reign of God (Luke 22:27; especially serving the poor and needy: Luke 10:22–37; 14:12–15; Matt. 5:42 and par.; 18:23–24; 25:31–46).

Here the text has a parenetic sense, bearing on the various "services," *diakoniai*, of the primitive communities. Because their *Sitz im Leben* was eucharistic, and because the thematics of sacrifice had been developed, it is only natural to suppose that this passage would have arisen under its influence. It would not be an authentic logion of the historical Jesus, then, as a goodly number of exegetes admit. As we shall see later, it was especially their reflection on Isaiah 53 that made it possible for the first Christians to read Christ's death as a sacrifice (Acts 8:32–35; Phil. 2:6–11; cf. Acts 3:13, 26; 4:27, 30). Jesus' words and deeds at his farewell meal were interpreted along the lines of Isaiah 53; after his death and resurrection, the community understood that the meaning of that meal had really been sacrifice to God. They understood that this Jesus, who had given himself all his life, here in his death was giving himself totally and completely. And so the eucharistic texts are altogether clear about this theological understanding: "This is my body, to be surrendered," they have Jesus say; "this is my blood to be shed." These would not be utterances of the historical Jesus, then, but an expression of a theology developed by the primitive communities, in a eucharistic context.

The parallel in Luke 22:27 includes no soteriological addition. It simply reads: "I am in your midst as the one who serves you." The addition "To give his life in ransom for the many," is peculiar to Mark, and belongs to his particular theological code.

The context is clear: "You know how among the Gentiles those who seem to exercise authority lord it over them" (Mark 10:42; cf. Luke 22:25). "It cannot be like that with you. Anyone among you who aspires to greatness must serve the rest" (Mark 10:43; cf. v. 44; cf. Luke 22:26). "The Son of Man has not come to be served but to serve" (Mark 10:45a; cf. Luke 22:27). The sequence could not be more transparent; there is nothing extraneous whatever. The disciple must invert the order of the world, because this is what the Son of Man does, and he is the example for his disciples. The addition of "give his life in ransom" (*lutron*) is a later interpolation, in function of the interpretation of Jesus' life and death as a sacrifice offered to God.

This passage, then, important as it is theologically, provides no special insight into the consciousness of the historical Jesus.

4. Nor does the text of Mark 10:38 or Matthew 20:22—"Can you drink the cup I shall drink?"—seem to offer any evidence of Jesus' foreknowledge of his manner of death. According to traditional imagery, the "cup" could mean a happy ending (Psalm 16:5–6; 23:5) or a tragic one (Psalm 11:6), especially when it implied the divine anger (Jer. 25:15–29; Isa. 51:17, 22; Ezek. 22:31–34). Here the cup is presented as a preliminary to glory. As we shall see later, the most likely meaning does not concern death, but the great trial in which the messiah and his enemies will be locked in combat.

5. Another passage that has been said to evidence Jesus' foreknowledge of his end is the parable of the property owner's only son, slain by the tenant farmers (Matt. 21:33–46; Mark 12:1–12; Luke 20:9–19). This powerful parable, however, does not refer to Jesus' death, but is a stern warning to the religious authorities (the tenant farmers in the vineyard of the Lord) to abandon their plot to liquidate Jesus. Jesus charges them with Israel's responsibility for the extermination of the prophets (Matt. 5:11–12 and par.; 23:29–36 and par.). In plotting to kill the son of the owner of the land, they are betraying the mission they have from God to be the guides of the people.

6. The prophecy of the shepherd who is struck, so that the sheep are dispersed (Mark 14:27; Matt. 26:31) is adduced by some scholars as an indica-

tion that the historical Jesus was aware of his coming death. Jesus cites Zechariah 13:7, and prophesies his own death:

> Your faith in me shall be shaken, for Scripture has it, "I will strike the shepherd and the sheep will be dispersed" [Zech. 13:7]. But after I am raised up, I will go to Galilee ahead of you [Mark 14:27–28].

But a considerable number of exegetes are of the opinion that the passage from Zechariah was introduced later by the primitive community, which was undergoing a severe trial in the form of the dispersal of the apostles (see Dodd, 42). The whole context, with its "after I am raised up" and "I will go to Galilee ahead of you," is redolent of the typical mannerisms of the oldest paschal tradition.

7. Another passage open to interpretation in terms of the historical Jesus' prophetic awareness of his violent end is the one that recounts a woman's anointing Jesus' head with "perfume made from expensive aromatic nard" (Mark 14:3–9; cf. Matt. 26:6–13 and John 12:1–8). And Jesus says:

> Let her alone. Why do you criticize her? She has done me a kindness. The poor you will always have with you and you can be generous to them whenever you wish, but you will not always have me. She has done what she could. By perfuming my body she is anticipating its preparation for burial [Mark 14:6–8].

To bury a body without anointing it was to treat it with the greatest dishonor. The woman has honored Jesus by anointing him in anticipation of his burial.

The pioneers of *Formgeschichte*, such as Dibelius and Bultmann, have demonstrated that what we are dealing with here is the later insertion of an already existing text: Mark 14:3–7. Underlying the account is a polemic within the community between those in favor of caring for the poor and those who had some objection against it. It is easier to grasp that the reference to Jesus' burial must date from after Jesus' resurrection if we attend to the following verse (Mark 14:9), with its typically postpaschal, ecclesial coloration: "I assure you, wherever the good news is proclaimed throughout the world, what she has done will be told in her memory." (See Bultmann, *Geschichte*, 37; Dibelius, *Formgeschichte*, 54, 58, 178–179.)

8. I have already considered the episode of Gethsemani (Matt. 26:36–46; Mark 14:32–42; Luke 20:40–46). As we have seen, there is no need to interpret Jesus' temptation as one of fear in the face of imminent death. What instills such great fear in Jesus is the approach of the great combat between the "children of light," or the disciples of the messiah, and the "children of darkness," the enemies of the messiah.

9. Jesus' last words on the cross (Mark 15:34; Matt. 27:46) bear all the earmarks of historical authenticity. First, they are preserved in Hebrew: *Lama sabachthani?* Secondly, Luke and John omit them. As we know, Luke and

John were written after the divinity of Jesus was a received datum. Indeed, John erects the doctrine into the very theme of his gospel. It is understandable, then, that Luke would replace these words, which come from Psalm 22:2, with words from another psalm: "Father, into your hands I commend my spirit" (Luke 23:46; Psalm 31:6). John 16:32 can be understood as an effort to avoid misunderstandings about Jesus' apparent abandonment on the cross:

> An hour is coming . . .
> when you will be scattered and each will go his way,
> leaving me quite alone.
> (Yet I can never be alone;
> the Father is with me) [John 16:32].

But we must take the last words of Jesus according to the first two synoptics absolutely seriously if we are interested in the actual consciousness of the historical Jesus. True, they are the opening words of a psalm, and a psalm that expresses not only the deep affliction of an innocent victim of oppression, but also his consolation in God, to the point of ending with a blessing pronounced on coming generations. But there is nothing to indicate that Jesus was simply praying a psalm. The text speaks to us of a rending, wrenching cry from out of the hell of the experience of the divine absence. The Father, with whom Jesus has lived in filial intimacy, the Father he has proclaimed as being of infinite goodness, the Father whose reign he has announced and anticipated in his praxis of liberation, now abandons him. It is not we who say this. It is Jesus.

Jesus, however, does not abandon God. Deep in the inmost recesses of his human soul, a person is suffering a paroxysm of hopelessness. Deprived of any personal title to God's support—such as fidelity, or the struggle he has waged for God's reign in the situation of his time, or the risks he has so willingly run, or the debasing process of the capital torture now visited upon him—Jesus is utterly empty before God. He can give God nothing now. And yet, though he sees the very earth slip from beneath his feet, still does he trust in his God, and still he cries out, perhaps without consciously adverting to the paradoxical trust it implies: "My God, my God" (Mark 15:34). His cry is a mighty one (Luke 23:46).

Here we have the greatest trial Jesus ever faced, ever lived. We might put it this way: "Has all my committed endeavor been in vain, then? Has all been but sweet illusion? Everything is finished now—and will there be no meaning for the human drama in any of it? Am I not the messiah after all?" The things that went on in Jesus' mind, his so human mind, devastated him, undid him utterly. Here he hangs, then, naked, helpless, totally empty before Mystery.

And what is his reaction? Does he grasp for one last, consoling thought, one last warranty and assurance of his being, his value? Nothing of the kind. He abandons himself to Mystery, truly the nameless Mystery. This alone will be his hope and security. He grasps at nothing whatsoever but—God.

Jesus' absolute hope and trust are intelligible only against the backdrop of his absolute despair. Where despair has abounded, hope can more abound. And because Jesus' hope was infinite, because his reliance was rooted in the Infinite alone, infinite too was his despair. Jesus' human greatness consisted in being able to bear up under so mighty a trial. No death need ever be absolutely solitary. It is, when one focuses it on one's own "I." But of itself it is an opportunity for surrender to a Greater. It is an opportunity for total surrender. If Jesus had had anything left inside—anything at all, some last certainty, some last, faint glimmer of messianic consciousness—his surrender could not have been complete. He would have been relying on himself. He would have been for-himself. He would not have been completely for-God. But he was totally emptied. Now he could be totally filled. This is called resurrection.

Christology itself, as well as the christological theme of the messianic consciousness of Jesus on his historical life pilgrimage, must, it seems to me, begin with Mark 15:34. Here is where we have to decide whether we accept or not, whether we take seriously or not, the radical fact of the incarnation of God as God's "humanization to the hilt," as the complete and total divine emptying in the sense of Philippians 2, including a deprivation of the divine attributes. By the incarnation, God becomes genuinely other. Hence we can speak theologically of Jesus' real, genuine humanity as being the divinity itself, the godhead present, and not merely the instrument of a divinity that holds itself substantially aloof, untouchable, and outside history. The Word *became* flesh, dwelling among us (John 1:14), pitching a tent in the mortal shadows of our life.

HOW HAD JESUS PICTURED THE OUTCOME?

The question we now broach is more usually formulated: How did Jesus interpret his death? But as we have seen, there is no historically authentic textual evidence for a consciousness or knowledge on the part of the historical Jesus of his approaching death. I am of the opinion that it was only on the cross that Jesus realized that his end was at hand—that he was really going to die. Then that great cry tears forth from the depths of his abandonment, almost like a cry of disappointment. And he surrenders to "my God." The Lukan, "Father, into your hands, I commend my spirit" (Luke 23:46), is a beautiful expression of Jesus' last interior disposition—absolute surrender, nothing but surrender.

Then what *had* Jesus expected? If we wish to have a picture of what he had actually expected—with all the vagueness and uncertainty attaching to an image constructed on the evidence we have—we must first attend to the following points.

1. Jesus preached not himself, but the reign of God. His word of hope was the reign of God: a sinful, corrupt world and humanity really transfigured, reconciled, and healed to the root by the coming of God. The reign of God did not mean another world, but this world, at last fully under God's sway, a world

in which Yahweh becomes present, and in which all that is adverse, malign, mortal, antidivine, and antihuman is fled. It is this hope, bursting up out of the furthest utopian depths of the heart and of history, that becomes the object of Jesus' preaching and proclamation.

2. The kingdom was at hand now (Mark 1:15; Matt. 3:17), indeed it was in our midst (Luke 17:21). This is Jesus' second great innovation. It was not enough to proclaim a utopia. The utopia was becoming "topian," topical, here-and-now. There is One who is mightier than the mighty, and this One resolves to intervene and have done with the sinister, rebellious character of the world (see Mark 3:27). The tone of Jesus' preaching, the extremely difficult demands he makes, his appeals for conversion, all ring with the imminent irruption of the reign of God, which is already at work in the world, and which will soon manifest itself in all its fullness.

3. Jesus understands himself not only as the herald of this exhilarating news (Mark 1:15), but as the vehicle and agent of its actualization: "If it is by the finger of God that I cast out devils, then the reign of God is upon you" (Luke 11:20). This is one of the best authenticated logia in the Gospels. So intimate is the identification Jesus feels between the reign of God and his own person, that he lays down attachment to that person as a requirement for membership in the community of God's reign (Luke 12:8-9). What the reign of God is in the concrete is revealed in his own praxis, in his "pro-existence," his being-for-others, his free and liberated inauguration of a process of liberation that provokes conflict with the social and personal rigidity of the historical agents of his time.

4. The historical Jesus moved about in the cultural atmosphere of his contemporaries. As his code, his key to the interpretation of the times, he adopted one of the prevailing world systems, the apocalyptical, and especially its concept of the reign of God and the imminence of the divine intervention. Many of his indisputably authentic logia spring from the apocalyptical mentality of the time: Luke 22:29-30; Matt. 19:28; Mark 13:30, 10:23, etc.

And among these logia we have two passages of basic importance for an insight into Jesus' consciousness. Both of them occur in the context of the last supper that the Lord celebrated among us:

> "I solemnly assure you, I will never again drink of the fruit of the vine until the day when I drink it new in the reign of God" [Mark 14:25].
>
> "I have greatly desired to eat this Passover with you before I suffer. I tell you, I will not eat again until it is fulfilled in the kingdom of God."
>
> Then taking a cup he offered a blessing in thanks and said: "Take this and divide it among you; I tell you, from now on I will not drink of the fruit of the vine until the coming of the reign of God."
>
> ". . . I for my part assign to you the dominion my Father has assigned to me. In my kingdom you will eat and drink at my table, and you will sit on thrones judging the twelve tribes of Israel" [Luke 22:15-18, 29-30].

As noted above, the Last Supper has an eminently eschatological meaning. It symbolizes and anticipates God's great and everlasting feast day, to be celebrated in the new order of things, the reign of God. As we shall see later, the bread and wine did not, on this level, symbolize the body and blood of Jesus to be sacrificed. This the primitive community will discover, once it has been through the living experience of Jesus' death and resurrection. With the historical Jesus, the bread and wine simply constituted the meal. But in a Jewish meal the bread and wine symbolized the heavenly banquet. And so it is altogether logical that Jesus would say: "I . . . assign to you the dominion [of the reign of God]. . . . You will eat and drink at my table." The bread and wine symbolized the feast of God's reign.

Neither of these texts has any organic connection with the life of the church. Their only connection is with Jesus. Indeed it is strange that they are preserved without theological interpretation on the part of the primitive community. And so we may quite confidently conclude that the eschatological mentality ascribed to Jesus has a historical basis, for which the first Christian theologians maintained a certain respect.

The apocalyptical code was admirably suited for conveying the utopian element—for translating the totalizing, universal dimension of liberation. This is what ultimately matters, not the linguistic, oniric, and cultural instrumentality that is the vehicle of that dimension.

According to these passages, then, Jesus was filled with the ebullience of the imminence of God's reign. He eventually came to realize that it was not the reign of God, but death that was in store for him, and this is what tore from his breast that shout on the cross, becoming the foundation of his total surrender to God. Now he saw all his models of the reign of God, and of his notions of his own activity in relationship to that reign, in shambles at his feet. But he was above his models and his notions, he was greater than his imaginings, and did not succumb to them, but maintained his fidelity to God.

5. One of the crucial elements of the apocalyptical system was the notion of the great trial, the great temptation. We have it in the apocalyptical passages of the New Testament, including the Apocalypse of Saint John (Book of Revelation). According to this theme, at the end of the ages, when the reign of God is about to burst upon the world, there will be one last great encounter between the messiah and his enemies. The demon himself will be the instigator of the great temptation. One must be well armed against it, lest one fall. And if it were not for the fact that God will intervene, even the good would succumb. The messiah will be persecuted, will be subjected to extreme hardship. But at the very moment when the trial has reached its paroxysm, God will intervene, deliver the messiah, and inaugurate his reign.

K. G. Kuhn ("Jesus in Gethsemani") has shown most compellingly that this is the conception we find as the backdrop for Jesus' temptation in Gethsemani. This temptation did not consist in any internal hesitations on Jesus' part, or in any uncertainty about the outcome. It consisted in his realization that the great trial was about to begin, with all the perils it would entail, including the danger of falling. In the Our Father, the expression "Lead us not into temptation" refers to this apocalyptic temptation at the end of the ages, when all the cards have been played and everything is about to be decided.

This too is the context in which many of the other better-attested logia of the historical Jesus are most easily situated. For instance, we hear Jesus say, "I have a baptism to receive. What anguish I feel till it is over!" (Luke 12:50). Or Jesus asks James and John, "Can you drink the cup I am to drink of?" (Matt. 20:22; Mark 10:38). The horizon against which these utterances are made is that of the great temptation.

Meanwhile, for Jesus the most important thing was to stay faithful to the Father: "But let it be as you would have it, not as I" (Mark 14:36 and par.).

Did Jesus expect his death? He perceived its possibility, surely. After all, he could scarcely have failed to observe the machinations of the religious authorities, who were weaving their toils around him. But this does not seem to have constituted a major problem for him. He goes on with his preaching with the same sovereignty, and the same invective, as if nothing were happening. He knows he is in his Father's hands, that Father with whom he feels himself to be on such terms of intimacy, and whose will he seeks to do always. The Father would save him from any merely personal danger. But the great temptation, the tremendous and dreadful trial, was another matter. Many of his own would fall away, and the messiah himself would pass through terrible tribulations. This is why he lay terror-stricken in the Garden of Gethsemani, beseeching his Father to let this cup pass.

But now, hanging on the cross, Jesus sees that he is about to die. He can forget about the great temptation now. Now he knows that his Father wishes his death. And his last cry is the expression of this last great crisis. But the Lukan and Johannine last words of Christ—"Father, into your hands I commend my spirit" (Luke 23:46), and "Now it is finished" (John 19:30)—manifest Jesus' surrender to his Father, not in defeat and helplessness, but in freedom.

AN ATTEMPT AT A RECONSTRUCTION OF JESUS' HISTORICAL PATH

The text of the New Testament in its present form, as has been shown above, is so permeated with theological interpretation that a complete, and completely reliable, reconstruction of the life of the historical Jesus is impossible. The historical Jesus is accessible to us only by way of the Christ of our faith. In other words, between the historical Jesus and ourselves come the interpretations that evolved out of the particular interests of the first Christians. This is an objective fact, and unchangeable.

But faith does not require the reconstruction of a historical system for its validity and vitality. Faith need only know that the interpretations to which it is heir rest on a generally valid historical basis: Jesus lived, preached, proclaimed the eschatological visitation of God to humanity; he encountered opposition, was tried and sentenced, and was liquidated; then the apostles testified that they had seen him alive again, alive with a divine, eternal life. For faith, the historical minutiae of the various stages of this human journey are important, but not decisive. The community of faith will take an interest in critical studies, and encourage them, but will not let its unconditional attachment to Jesus Christ depend on concepts in the heads of historians or on the latest theological hypotheses of Christian thinkers. Theological hypotheses are of course important. Generally speaking they nourish the life of concrete faith; they actualize faith and make it come alive in the world. But the faith community does not depend on them for the constitution of its faith. It avails itself of them in order to develop, in order to "give an account of its hope" (1 Pet. 3:15), to endow the free adherence of faith with conscious rational structures.

As a consequence, all attempts at a reconstruction of Jesus' historical pilgrimage will have only a precarious, hypothetical value, and my own will be no exception. Of course, every generation will make the attempt, from out of the particular existential situation of its own culture and its own interpretation of the New Testament texts. All faith, concretely, draws its life from such representations. The problem is not whether to make these representations or not make them. We always make them. The problem is *how* to make them. The accent is on *how* our particular way of life, our anxieties, and our situation in society and the world present themselves. There are as many interpretations of the historical Jesus, then, as there are ways of historicizing Christian faith. Nor should any Christian seek to avoid a confrontation with the texts of the New Testament. Flight would be in vain in any case. We must all submit to these texts, erecting them into the critical instance, the vital criterion, of our interpretations and our lives. An interpretation that ignores this critical task cannot legitimately ask for communitarian, ecclesial recognition.

These, then, are the limits within which I now trace, in rapid outline, what it seems to me Jesus' historical life must have been.

1. Jesus was from Nazareth, a village of Galilee. His family was religious, and carefully observed both the law and the sacred traditions. It was his family who initiated Jesus into the great experience of God. We owe the one who was given to us, and given to us to know, not only to the mysterious designs of providence, but to his family. God employs no superfluous mediations; all of them are there for the enhancement of history.

An important practice in every observant Jewish household was the reading of and meditation on the sacred books. Nor was this mere "piety." It was a real school of life. It taught Jews to interpret life and history in the light of God. They strove to understand past and present alike in the light of the word of God.

2. This was the atmosphere in which, we must suppose, Jesus first learned to interpret the signs of his age theologically. (We have no historical documents to this effect, but literary documents are not the only source of history. The actual rhythm of life is the principal source of historical knowledge.) It was a time of political and religious oppression. For centuries the country had been under

foreign domination. This scarcely seemed to be the meaning of the divine promises, with their language of Israel's sovereignty and the reign of Yahweh. And the people lived under another yoke, as well: that of a petty interpretation of the law and of the will of God. Jesus' sovereignty with respect to the law and religious tradition did not drop into his head out of the sky. It was his whole manner of being, and had been growing within him from childhood, from the days of his upbringing. The life of young Jesus of Nazareth must have been filled with a profound, unquestioned, intimate, warm experience of God, whom he called his "daddy," *Abba.*

3. The cultural atmosphere generated by the political and religious contradictions of his time was ideally suited to the apocalyptic spirit. The times breathed decadence, wickedness, and the rebellion of this world. The world had been possessed by diabolical forces, inimical to God. The Romans with their paganization, the all-pervasive legalism, the Herodians and their machinations, were but puppets on a stage, playing out a drama whose producer-director was the evil one. But God had resolved to intervene and put an end to all this. The Son of Man would come to the clouds of his majesty bearing the judgment of God, to exalt the just, punish the evil, and inaugurate a new order. The name given to this new order rang with boundless hope and trembling anticipation on the part of the whole people (Luke 3:15): it was called the "reign of God." And now it was time to prepare for its imminent coming. One must be ready for judgment and salvation. Jesus, as a person of his times, essentially shared these hopes.

The biblical scholar must keep in mind that apocalypticism was a system articulating the utopian depths of the human heart. Its bizarre symbolism, and especially the signs it proposed by which the dramatic, dazzling end would be recognized, breathed hope and joy. The Lord would come, and would conquer. This is the symbolism that translated, for Jesus' age, the inexhaustible optimism at the heart of all "religion"—that matrix of hope, salvation, and reconciliation.

4. The adult Jesus of Nazareth became attracted to the preaching of John the Baptist. John proclaimed the imminent judgment of God, and hence the urgency of conversion. We do not know that Jesus was a disciple of John, but neither do we know that he was not. John probably did have a circle of disciples who followed him and helped him administer the baptism of repentance (Mark 2:18; Matt. 11:1–2; John 1:35, 3:22). According to John the Evangelist's Gospel, Jesus, too, went out to baptize (John 3:22–36; cf. 4:1–2). We do not know whether he did so independently or as John's assistant, but we do know that Jesus' disciples were recruited from John's circle (John 1:35–51). We also know that Jesus embraced and proclaimed the core of John's message: that the time for repentance was at hand. This meant two things: that all Israel, indeed all humanity, was evil in the sight of God; and that doing penance would prepare the people to receive God's gift of salvation. For God was now very near. John's preaching was regarded by Jesus as coming "from God" (Luke 20:4).

5. The account of Jesus' baptism by John is charged with the theology of a community that had witnessed the glory of the one raised from the dead. Nevertheless, it is clear that, on the occasion of his baptism by John, Jesus underwent a decisive prophetic experience. He came to the conviction that the history of salvation was linked to his person, and he parted ways with John. John preached judgment; Jesus preached the gospel of salvation and joy. John was a rigid ascetic; Jesus was accused of being a glutton, a drunkard, and the keeper of bad company in the form of tax collectors and sinners. The image of the child playing the flute in the village square was intended to convey the difference between Jesus and John, whose lifestyles were in conformity with their respective messages: John's message was God's stern judgment; Jesus' was the glad news of salvation (Matt. 11:16–19; Luke 7:31–35).

6. Let me attempt to capsulize Jesus' exhilarating proclamation. (a) The longed-for kingdom was approaching, and (b) the way to prepare for it was by the faith in this wonderful news and by conversion, for (c) it would burst upon the world at any moment now, bringing (d) salvation to all, especially to sinners, because (e) God was a father of infinite goodness who loved all without distinction, even the ungrateful and the wicked, although God had a preferential love for the poor, the weak, the insignificant, and the sinful. Finally, (f) all this was conditioned on adherence to himself, Jesus, the herald, anticipator, and actualizer of the reign of forgiveness and salvation.

7. This message of liberation was conveyed by Jesus' free, untrammeled word, and by his freeing, liberating actions. Parables drawn from life, maxims in the wisdom genre, and a style of speech that was intelligible to all, were part and parcel of Jesus' way of communicating. But the ultimate key to the way in which he communicated his conviction that the reign of God was at the gates was his praxis: he liberated through miraculous, symbolic acts, whose meaning consisted not so much in a revelation of his divine power, but in concretizing in actual history, and in a humble, lowly life, the dynamic reign of God. He performed his activity of liberation in the main by de-absolutizing and de-mystifying laws and traditions that had become lethal—that hindered life from being human life, and that robbed the people of its capacity to hear the living word of God.

The thrust of Jesus' praxis was not toward particular areas of life, such as worship, or ritual, or devotional religion, but toward life as a whole, understood as a service of love to be rendered to others. To stand before God at every moment, and not only when one goes to pray or offer sacrifice, is Jesus' basic demand. We must love others in the same spirit with which we love God. But Jesus did not moralize upon life. He generated a whole new quality of life. The question was an ontological one, not a moral one. Morality is a consequence, or reflex, of ontology.

8. What sustained Jesus' message and praxis ("He has done everything well!"—Mark 7:37) was his deep experience of God. Jesus' God was no longer the stiff, distant God of the Torah. Jesus' God was a God and Father of infinite goodness, eager to be of service to every human being, exhibiting gracious,

benevolent compassion for all, especially the ungrateful and the wicked (Luke 6:35). Jesus reverses this God. He prays to his Father, he asks his Father for blessings and favors. At the same time, he feels a profound intimacy with God, to the point of feeling himself to be, and calling himself, God's son. He feels that God acts through him. God's kingdom is made manifest in Jesus' action and life. His dining with sinners, his association with the unclean and marginalized, is not humanitarianism, but a way of concretizing God's love and unrestricted forgiveness with regard to all who consider themselves lost. By joining those whose self-image is that of persons crushed and marginalized, Jesus instills in them a certitude that God is with them, that God accepts them and forgives them.

It is in terms of this living love for God that we can understand the paradox of Jesus' life. On the one hand he is liberal with regard to the law, religious tradition, and the social and religious mores of the day; at the other hand he demonstrates an extreme ethical radicalism, as in the Sermon on the Mount. This paradox is easy to explain in the light of an experience of a God of love and goodness. Love knows no limits. To attempt to confine it would be to kill it. Love is demanding. It must love each and every human being. For the sake of love like that, Jesus is willing to come in conflict with the law and the traditions that put obstacles in the path of love, law and traditions that curb love. Jesus is against nothing, not even the law, not even pharisaical piety. His objections arise out of a new project for human existence, an existence understood in the light of a new experience of God. It is this experience that moves him to subject all that he encounters to a purifying, refining critique.

9. The reign of God will not come by magic. It is a pro-position, seeking the free re-sponse of men and women. And so the reign of God is historical, and structured personally, though not exclusively personally. The reign of God will not be forced on anyone, for the Father is a God not of violence, but of love and freedom. Jesus therefore, with the same forcefulness with which he proclaims the good news of the reign of God, preaches the urgency of conversion. You cannot have one without the other. Indeed, conversion is not only a sine qua non for God's reign, it is that reign itself, already beginning to be realized in human lives.

10. Jesus' preaching had an impact. The masses converged on him to hear his new teaching, and to feel the gladness that it occasioned. Meanwhile, he made demands on his hearers, and eventually he had to pay for the privilege of thinking and acting in the way that he did. He eventually provoked a deep crisis in the people and in his followers. Slowly but surely, he was becoming a failure. Jesus observed this himself: "Blest is that man who finds no stumbling block in me" (Luke 7:23, esp. vv. 18–23; Matt. 11:6). The masses withdrew. Then the disciples. Finally even the apostles threatened to abandon him (see John 6:67). Then there is the so-called Galilean crisis (Mark 9:19–32; Luke 9:41–45). Jesus realizes that there is a plot against his life. Luke 9:51 tells us that Jesus "firmly resolved"—literally, "set his face"—to go to Jerusalem. And Mark comments: "The disciples were on the road going up to Jerusalem, with Jesus walking in

the lead. Their mood was one of wonderment, while that of those who followed was fear" (Mark 10:32). There, in Jerusalem, in the temple, according to a prevalent apocalyptical belief, the reign of God would burst forth in all its dazzling splendor.

11. Jesus must have seen the crisis coming and resigned himself to it. He finds himself more and more alone. Grave accusations are lodged. He is a false prophet (Matt. 27:62–64; John 7:12). He is mentally disturbed (Mark 3:24). He is a fraud (Matt. 27:63). He is subversive (Luke 23:2, 14). He is possessed (Mark 3:22; John 7:20). He is a heretic (John 8:48). And so on and so forth. He consoles himself with the thought that "no prophet is without honor except in his native place" (Mark 6:4; Matt. 13:57; Luke 4:24; John 4:44).

These crises must have had an effect on Jesus' self-image. Jesus was not "impassible," wafting sovereignly above the course of history. Initially he thought of himself as God's eschatological herald and prophet, and he proclaimed salvation and preached conversion. Now, in the face of this resistance thrown up against him, he realized that he could come to a traumatic end. He did not basically alter his behavior. He continued to preach with the same courage as before, still trusting in the human capacity for devotedness and conversion. But now he began to see himself as the suffering just man of Old Testament and apocalyptical theology alike. Loyal to God and to the law, the just one will be persecuted, humiliated, perhaps even murdered. But God will exalt him. This figure of the suffering just one, the suffering prophet, fits in very well with the atmosphere of apocalypticism of the time.

The death of the just one in expiation for the sins of others was a rabbinical, and not an apocalyptical theological theme. According to the rabbis, a martyr need not be just (see 2 Macc. 7:32), not even to atone for the sins of others (see apocryphal 4 Macc. 6:28; 17:22). Even a criminal under capital sentence could perform an act of expiation, through his free acceptance of his death.

It does not seem that Jesus considered himself the suffering servant of Isaiah (against the theses of Cullmann and Jeremias). According to F. Hahn, and especially Wiard Popkes, Jesus gave himself up willingly, but without reference to the song of the servant in Isaiah 53—that is, without explicit consciousness of being the suffering servant. Most probably in the consciousness of the historical Jesus he was the eschatological prophet and suffering just one (Lothar Ruppert). But this consciousness developed only gradually in his life, as he began to encounter opposition and to assess and accept his situation.

12. It is surely clear from the general tone of the Gospels that it was God, and not the situation Jesus happened to be in, that gave him his direction and orientation. His activity was spontaneous action, not reaction to the initiatives of others. In all things he was disposed to do the will of his Father, with whom he felt himself to be in intimate union. But his Father's will was not some sort of drama playing in his head, with a predetermined, foreordained scenario, so that he would know everything ahead of time. If he had had previous knowledge of everything, his preaching, his insistence on conversion, like the rest of his whole, earnest commitment, would have been nothing more than one, long

"as if." It would have been "just pretend." His death, too, would have been mere play-acting. But Jesus was a *homo viator*, a pilgrim like ourselves. Of course, as the eschatological prophet and just one, he possessed an unprecedented sense of the divine, and of the concrete will of God. But he did not know the ordinations of that will a priori. He had to go in search of them, in all fidelity and with all interior purity. He found the expression of the divine will in the concrete life he led as an itinerant prophet—in the intimacy of his group, in his disputes with the Pharisees and in his other encounters, and in prayer and meditation, in which God surprised him as much in the lilies of the field as in the reading of the scriptures. What the will of God would be for each moment, Jesus could not know a priori. But he could learn it, in the ordinary events of every day—in the unforeseeable, contingent, fortuitous events of history.

The earnestness of Jesus' search for the divine will, the intensity and intimacy of his union with God, led him always to accept that will, whether in the joy of the apostles' enthusiastic return from their preaching (Mark 6:30–31; Matt. 14:22), in his flight from those who sought to kill him (Luke 4:30; John 8:59, 10:39), or even on the cross, face to face with death. It could not have always been easy for him to accept the will of God, which might destroy the notions he had formed of the kingdom (see Luke 22:15–29; Mark 14:25), and we clearly see this in his temptation in Gethsemani. But he achieved what was most important: to be entirely attentive to, and obedient to, the divine will, and this to the death. And so just as Jesus' whole existence had been a pro-existence, a being-for-others, so also the sufferings he bore must be understood as accepted before God in the form of an exigency of the cause Jesus represented, and accepted in fidelity to all humankind. For it was for the sake of all of human beings that he was a prophet.

13. Failing in Galilee, where he had been conducting his activity, Jesus went to Jerusalem. There he expected to see the complete irruption of the reign of God and the victory of his cause. He entered Jerusalem, in the company of his disciples, and went to the temple, because it was there that the reign of God was to manifest itself:

> He entered Jerusalem and went into the temple precincts. He inspected everything there, but since it was already late in the afternoon, he went out to Bethany accompanied by the Twelve [Mark 11:11].

It seems to me that we are dealing with a crucial text here. It introduces a caesura into the general context, and constitutes one of the great problems of New Testament exegesis. It becomes intelligible, however, in light of the consciousness of the prophet from Nazareth. He enters the temple. He inspects everything there. For him the atmosphere is electric. The kingdom could burst forth at any moment, from any part of the temple. And nothing happens. And so he leaves for Bethany, to lodge with his friends Lazarus, Martha, and Mary.

He returns the following day. Now the Gospels recount the purification of the temple. What is transpiring here? Does Jesus' action spring simply from a spirit of severity and indignation? In my view, Jesus' action here is performed in view of his expectation of the imminent descent of the reign of God. The reign of God fails to come in the temple because the temple has become unclean, and thus unworthy of God. It must be purified. Then the proper conditions will be present for the glorious manifestation of God to all, and the inauguration of God's dominion over all things.

But the account of the purification, in the Markan version, concludes with almost the same words as the preceding account: "When evening drew on, Jesus and his disciples went out of the city" (Mark 11:19). Once more one of Jesus' conceptions is destroyed. This interior process of destruction and building anew, of death and resurrection, is the ongoing process of human life, and Jesus' life is no exception. Human beings live by interpreting, and interpret by living. We construct a meaning for the world, and the task of faith is everlastingly to wrench free of it, so as to be free for God and God's daily newness. Jesus is par excellence a person of faith and hope. If faith does not consist merely in an intellectual assent to salvific truths and facts, but, more basically, in a manner of living by which I continually surrender to God, so that now I live from, by, and in God, then Jesus was the believer par excellence. This is the sense in which Hebrews 12:2 says he is the *archegos* and *teleiotes* of faith—the one who begins and ends, he who per-fects, "does thoroughly," the faith. In other words, Jesus is the one who has believed in such wise as now to constitute the ultimate source of faith as such. And he is this because he himself has believed, has exercised the act of faith, even as the mighty exemplars of the Old Testament exercised faith; we read their apologia in the long, incomparable chapter 11 of the Letter to the Hebrews. Here is why he is called "faithful" in Hebrews 3:2, *pistos*, the one who has faith (cf. Heb. 2:13, 2:17, 5:8, where the obedience learned by Jesus is synonymous for faith).

Faith was the constant nourishment of the life of Jesus. Enlightened by his faith, he read in the events of his life experience the concrete will of God and accepted it.

14. In Gethsemani Jesus experienced the preludes of the great, eschatological temptation. Everything was clear now: the great moment had come when all would be decided. And Jesus feared that moment. "My heart is filled with sorrow to the point of death" (Mark 14:34). He prayed (Mark 14:32). He begged to be spared "this hour" (Mark 14:35): "*Abba* (O Father), you have the power to do all things. Take this cup away from me. But let it be as you would have it, not as I" (Mark 14:36). "This hour" and "cup" are technical expressions found in the apocalyptical vocabulary of the time.

Jesus leaves his place of prayer strengthened by his trial. Trustingly he surrenders to God's secret design. His situation is a perilous one indeed, but he trusts that God will deliver him.

15. The entire passion account is a tale of one "handing over" after another. Jesus is handed over to the Sanhedrin by Judas (Mark 14:10, 43:46). The Sanhedrin hands him over to Pilate (Mark 15:1, 10). Pilate hands him over to the soldiers (Mark 15:15). And the soldiers deliver him up to death (Mark

15:25). Finally God delivers him over to his fate, and he dies with a cry of abandonment on his lips (Mark 14:34). Jesus remains serene and sovereign throughout the process, and the Gospels take careful note of this. But Jesus' disposition is not one of stoicism. It is one of trusting, absolute surrender to God. Jesus follows the Mystery, wherever it may lead, and whatever it is.

16. What meaning did Jesus ascribe to his death? The one he ascribed to his life. Jesus understood life not as something to be lived and enjoyed for itself, but as something to be lived for service to others. *Diakonia* was one of Jesus' characteristic traits. Saint Mark sums it up appositely: "He has done everything well! He makes the deaf hear and the mute speak!" (Mark 7:37). And a modern theologian explains:

> Contemporary New Testament research is almost certainly correct in its insistence that Jesus himself did not understand his death as an expiatory sacrifice, as satisfaction, or as redemption. Nor was it his intention to redeem human beings precisely through his death. Redemption, in Jesus' mind, depended on human beings' acceptance of his God and of the manner of living for others that he preached and personally lived. In Jesus' mind, then, salvation and redemption did not depend on his future death, but on human beings' allowing themselves to be penetrated by the universally good God revealed by Jesus. This would surely lead men and women to a corresponding behavior vis-à-vis their neighbors, in an effort to free them, liberate them. In a word, redemption would come by way of a love exercised in actions, and sprung from a trusting faith in God (Gal. 5:6) [Kessler, *Erlösung*, 25].

Redemption, then, does not depend on some mathematical point in Jesus' life, not even on the moment of his death. It is Jesus' whole life that is redemptive. His death is redemptive only in its identity as part of his life. Jesus accepted his death as he accepted everything else—as coming from the hand of God. Of course, death has a qualitatively eminent anthropological significance, in that it constitutes the culmination of life. And therefore we can and must say that to Jesus his death represented the apex of his pro-existence, his being-for-others. In complete dedication and freedom, Jesus lived his death as surrender to God and human beings, whom he loved to the end (John 17:1).

Jesus' death represents the culmination of his whole life of service, then, and in this sense, and this sense alone, it possesses a human fullness such as to qualify it as having an intrinsic value. But the moment of Jesus' death does not exhaust Jesus' value, any more than it exhausts his salvific intent.

TRANSCENDENT MEANING OF JESUS' DEATH

The causes of Jesus' death were banal, to be sure—a concern for security, selfishness, "system sclerosis." His death, however, was in no way commonplace. In Jesus' death all his greatness shone forth. Jesus transformed oppression itself into a pathway of liberation. At a certain moment—that of the Galilean crisis—Jesus came to realize that he was engaged in a dramatic, life-and-death struggle. He was not unaware that John the Baptist had been executed (Mark 6:14–29). He was not ignorant of how the prophets before him had died (Matt. 23:37; Luke 13:33–34; Acts 2:23). He did not simply blunder ahead toward his death. He did not seek it, or wish it. The Gospels recount how he went into hiding (John 11:57, 12:36, 18:2; Luke 21:37), and avoided the Pharisees, who were harassing him (Mark 7:24, 8:13; cf. Matt. 12:15, 14:13). But like every "just one" he was ready to sacrifice his life if that was necessary to bear witness to his truth (John 18:37).

Of course, in his apocalyptical mentality he expected to be delivered by God from any really life-threatening situation. He was striving for the conversion of the Jews. But, isolated as he was, he had no intention of resigning himself to, or compromising with, any given situation merely in order to survive. He remained faithful to his truth to the end, heedless of any danger. He strode into danger with his eyes wide open, and embraced it. His was not the spirit of fatalism, but of freedom, of a liberty that is willing to risk life itself to testify to a message. "No one takes my life from me; I lay it down freely" (John 10:18).

Death is not retribution for Jesus, it is testimony. It is not fatality, but liberty. Jesus does not fear death, nor does he act out of a fear of death. He lives and acts despite death. If death must come, let it come, but the vitality and inspiration of his life is not the fear of death: it is commitment to his Father's will as that will is read in the concrete details of one's life, and in a commitment to a message of liberation for a world of brothers and sisters.

The prophet, the just one, as Jesus, who dies for justice and truth, denounces the wickedness of this world, and indicts all the closed systems, with their pretensions to a monopoly over truth and good. It is this monopolistic closure that is the "sin of the world." Christ died in consequence of this commonplace, all-pervasive sin: structured sin. His reaction did not fall within his enemies' scheme of things. A victim of oppression and violence, he nevertheless did not use violence and oppression to force himself on others. *Hate can kill, but it cannot define the meaning given by the victim to his or her own death* (Duquoc, *Christologie*, 204). Christ defined the sense of his death in terms of love, gift, and free sacrifice in behalf of his killers and all men and women. The dying prophet from Nazareth was the Son of God, too—a faith reality that shone forth as reality only after the resurrection. And yet, though Son of God, he made no use of the divine power that can change all situations. He bore no witness to a power of domination, for this is the diabolical side of power, this is the power that generates oppression and obstacles to communion. He bore witness to the true power of God, which is love, a love that liberates, establishes human beings in solidarity with one another, and opens them to the laborious process of liberation.

This love excludes all violence and oppression, even for the sake of imposing itself. Its effectiveness is not the effectiveness of violence. Violence changes situations, yes, but only by eliminating human beings. The perverse effectiveness of violence fails to free itself from the spirit of oppression. Love has its own efficacy, an efficacy that cannot immediately be seen and isolated—the courage to sacrifice one's very life for love, and the certitude that the future belongs to right, justice, love, and a communion of sisters and brothers, and not to oppression, revenge, and injustice.

It is not to be wondered at that, as the experience of past centuries as well as our own times has shown, the murderers of the prophets and the just become more and more violent as their downfall looms. Indeed the wicked are stripped of their very solidarity with one another, simply by the wickedness of their own injustice. There is a falling-out among killers, no honor among thieves. God does not act unless men and women, in their liberty, wish it. The reign of God is a process requiring the participation of human beings. If human beings refuse, it will not be by violence but by sacrificial love that they will continue to be invited to surrender: "And I—once I am lifted up from earth—will draw all men to myself" (John 12:32).

Christ's death, even apart from the light bestowed upon it in his resurrection, has a meaning consistent with his life. All who, like Jesus, demand more justice, more love, more respect for the rights of the oppressed, and more liberty for God, must expect opposition, and the possibility of their liquidation. Death is vanquished when it ceases to be the terrifying specter that prevents us from living and proclaiming the truth. Now death is accepted. It is simply inserted into the project of the just person and true prophet. It can be expected. It must be expected.

Jesus' greatness consists in having refused to yield to the spirit of comfort and convenience. Even on the cross, overwhelmed by a conviction of abandonment by the God he has so earnestly and steadfastly served, Jesus refuses to give over to resignation. He forgives, and he keeps believing and hoping. In the very paroxysm of defeat, he gives himself into the hands of his mysterious Father, in whom resides the ultimate meaning of the absurdity that is the death of the innocent one. At the nadir of despair and abandonment, Jesus finds the zenith of trust in and surrender to his Father. He has no foothold in himself or his accomplishments. In God alone is his support, in God alone can he place his hope. Here is a hope that transcends the bounds of death. Here is the perfect deed of liberation. Here Jesus has delivered himself entirely from himself, in order to be completely God's.

Socrates, as Bonhoeffer says, delivered us from dying, by his serenity and sovereignty. Christ does so much more, delivering us from death itself. Christ's death touched the furthest reaches of hopelessness. But his self-surrender for our sake and God's was so boundless, so complete, that it defeated death's very dominion. This is the meaning of resurrection, resurrection bursting forth from the very abyss of annihilation.

Chapter 5

Ultimate Meaning of the Death of Christ: Resurrection

The purpose of our reflections has been to afford an insight into the liberation process initiated by Jesus Christ in all dimensions of his life. For liberation is process, and as such will always have a note of partiality and incompleteness. The process is open. Where will it end? In what will it issue? What does it anticipate?

If Christ had confined himself to the process as such, of course, he would not have been proclaimed the universal liberator. His liberation would have been only partial, not total. True liberation, liberation worthy of the name, must have the notes of totality and universality as well. And the totality of liberation is in resurrection. In resurrection, the utopian truth of the reign of God becomes "topian." It becomes topical, it acquires "a local habitation and a name," in order to show that it is not trapped in an indefinite circularity of oppression-and-liberation, but issues in total, exhaustive liberation.

Resurrection is not a phenomenon of human biology—of cellular physiology, for example. Christ was not reanimated for the kind of life he had already had. Resurrection means the complete and definitive enthronement of human reality, spirit and body together, in the atmosphere of the divine. In other words, resurrection is complete hominization and liberation. In the person of the resurrected Jesus, history has reached its term. This is why resurrection can be presented as complete and total liberation for human nature. Death is vanquished now, and a new kind of human life has been inaugurated—one no longer ruled by the mechanisms of corruption and death, but vivified by the divine life itself.

The resurrection has a protest value, then. It protests the "justice" and "right" by which Christ was condemned. It protests the assignment of any merely immanent meaning to this world with its "law and order," for that "law and order" finally rejected the one whom God, by raising him, has endorsed. Thus the resurrection is the matrix of a liberative hope, a hope that surpasses and transcends a world that lives under the specter of death.

James Cone, acknowledged dean of the black theology of liberation, is right when he says:

[Jesus'] resurrection is the disclosure that God is not defeated by oppression but transforms it into the possibility of freedom. For men and women who live in an oppressive society this means that they do not have to behave as if *death* is the ultimate. God in Christ has set us free from death, and we can now live without worrying about social ostracism, economic insecurity, or political death. "In Christ the immortal God has tasted death and in so doing . . . destroyed death" (compare Hebrews 2:14ff.) [Cone, 210–11, citing Richardson, 60].

The one who was raised up is the one who was crucified. The liberator is the suffering servant, the oppressed one. To live liberation from death means no longer to permit death to have the last word in life, no longer to let death determine all our acts and attitudes through a fear of being dead. Jesus' resurrection has shown that living for truth and justice is not meaningless and senseless. It has shown that the oppressed and liquidated have a life reserved for them, the life that has now been manifested in Jesus Christ. They may take courage, then, and live the freedom of the daughters and sons of God, who are not subject to the inhibiting powers of death.

The evangelists were able to use the resurrection of Christ to reread the death of the prophet and martyr, Jesus of Nazareth. Now it was no longer a death like other deaths, not even the most heroic of them. It was the death of the Son of God, the one sent by the Father. Now everything was clear: the conflict waged by Jesus had not been a conflict merely between Jesus' freedom and the legalistic observance of the law: the conflict had been between the reign of corrupt humanity and the reign of God. The cross was not only the most ignominious torment of the time, it was the symbol of what human beings are capable of with their piety (for it was religious persons who murdered Jesus), with their fanatic zeal for God, with their closed dogmatism, and with revelation reduced to obsession with a text. This is why Christ's death seemed so repulsive and absurd to him. He had always lived for God (Heb. 5:7). But he accepted it nonetheless, transforming it into a sign of toilsome liberation from precisely what had occasioned the cross: self-sufficiency, closure, pettiness, and the spirit of revenge.

The resurrection is not only the event that glorifies and justifies Jesus Christ, his truth, and his attitudes. It is also the manifestation of what the reign of God is in its plenitude: the epiphany of the future that God has promised. It is the demonstration of what men and women can hope for, because it is God who has promised it to them.

The evangelists reflected in their Gospels all these dimensions, which they had discovered in the life and death of Christ in light of his resurrection. The Gospels give us facts, then, but they stamp these facts with a deep meaning, one that transcends pure, factual historicity. Were we to neglect to distinguish these two levels, the profound meaning of the life and death of Christ would seem abstract. It would not seem to have foundation and support in reality.

The discovery, in the resurrection, that the oppressed one was the liberator, occasioned a more meaningful reading of Jesus' infancy and later life. Jesus' birth, as the synoptics demonstrate so well, expresses the identification of the oppressed liberator with all the oppressed of the earth—with the shepherds, with the Holy Innocents, with the pagan Magi. From the very beginning, Jesus appears among the oppressed: "There was no room for them in the place where travelers lodged" (Luke 2:7). The social and economic poverty of Jesus' land is emphasized in Jesus' identification with the poor and downtrodden. For the primitive Christian community, who read and meditated on these accounts, this meant: Jesus' messiahship is bound up with humiliation. The humiliated and the wronged can take heart, then: the messiah is one of themselves. Indeed it is because of this—not in spite of this—that he is the messianic liberator. It is this precise outlook that is developed by the evangelists when they recount Jesus' public ministry, conducted as it was in such intimate association with the marginalized of his time. Along with their historical interest, then, the evangelists manifest a theological concern: Jesus identified himself with the suffering and downtrodden, and bore their burden, freeing them for a new solidarity.

Thus the whole of the life, activity, death, and resurrection of Christ acquires a liberative significance. To be sure, this meaning was already present in the bare facts and events themselves. But it was totally revealed only after the explosion of the resurrection. The resurrection enabled Jesus' followers to reread the same phenomena on a deeper level, and so to detect their profound, transcendent, exemplary, and universal significance.

Only when taken in conjunction with his life and death does Jesus' resurrection have a realistic meaning. Otherwise it becomes either pagan mythology, or a modern ideology of a future of reconciliation without the conversion of historical evils. In Jesus, resurrection means the victory of life, the victory of the rights of the oppressed, the victory of justice for the weak.

Chapter 6

Interpretations of Christ's Death by the Primitive Christian Communities

The death of Christ shook the community of his disciples. It not only frustrated their hopes, it uprooted their immature faith. Mark 15:50 (the disciples' flight), Luke 24:21 (on the road to Emmaus, two disciples discuss their disappointment in Jesus as the savior of Israel), and John 20:19 (the disciples' "fear of the Jews") all testify to this. The apostles did not tarry in Jerusalem after Christ's arrest and execution. Things would have been too difficult for them there. They might have been seized and thrown into prison. We read that the first postresurrection apparitions occurred in Galilee, and so we may assume that the apostles were back home again, plying their fishing trade, just as they had been doing a few years earlier, before they met Jesus.

In order to be able to interpret Jesus' death, the apostles had to have a special experience: the resurrection. Through Jesus' resurrection, the apostles realized that he had only seemed to be abandoned by God at death—that in actuality God had not abandoned him at all. His resurrection showed that God had been with him then, and was with him still. This is why the resurrection was seen as culminating in the ascension, the exaltation of the just one to the right hand of God and his enthronement in the realm of glory. God had justified Jesus, endorsing both him and his message.

The resurrection made the disciples a community again. It enabled Jesus' followers to bridge the chasm that death had brought with it and regain faith in the Lord. The church is born of faith: faith in Jesus' resurrection.

The problem was how to resolve the paradox of the curse of Jesus' death (Deut. 21:23: "God's curse rests on him who hangs on a tree") and his resurrection to glory. How could both occurrences have their origin in the selfsame God? How could the God who had abandoned Jesus on the cross now be shown to be at his side in the resurrection?

In order to respond to this question, the primitive church practiced theology,

69

and its theologizing took a good deal of time. Let us examine the steps leading from the Jewish-Christian prechurch to the plenitude of a Pauline theology.

COMMON DESTINY OF THE PROPHETS AND THE JUST: VIOLENT DEATH

In the years immediately following the death of Christ, there was a little group of Christians in Palestine who saw redemption as having been outlined by Jesus in a new way of life marked out for them and made feasible by his contacts with the world and with his fellow human beings. This new comportment consisted of universal love (implying love for one's enemies, mercy, renunciation of violence, and refusal to judge others), the preaching of the message of the reign of God, and hope in Jesus' imminent return as Daniel's "son of man."

This was the community of the *Spurchquelle*, or simply Q (*Quelle*), the "source"—meaning the earlier, no longer extant, written source of the Gospels of Matthew and Luke. These were Jewish Christians, faithful to their traditions and to the observance of every last jot and tittle of the Law (Matt. 5:18 and par.). They observed the temple worship, and as yet entertained no extra-Palestinian missionary intention. Of course they sought to convert Israel to the cause of Jesus Christ: then, they thought, all nations of the earth would come to Jerusalem of their own accord (see Isa. 2:2–5; Matt. 8:10 and par.).

The *Quelle*, unlike the Gospel of Mark (the other main source of the Gospels of Matthew and Luke), consisted entirely of Jesus' sayings and parables. It contained no account of the passion, either because this was presupposed as known, or because no interpretation of Jesus' death had as yet been developed. Its central themes, as we have seen, were identical with the central interests of the historical Jesus himself: the coming of the reign of God (Luke 11:20 and par.; Matt. 13:31–52) and how one can be its subject (Matt 8:11); the imminent return of the Son of Man; and therefore the urgency of conversion in preparation for the impending end. This community understood Jesus as the last messenger, the eschatological prophet, of the reign of God.

The death of Christ was understood by this group as the death that awaited any prophet (Luke 11:49–51; 13:14; 1 Thess. 2:14; Acts 7:51–53). The murder and liquidation of prophets was part and parcel of the pattern of the whole history of Israel, and no exception had been made for Jesus. Thus Jesus' death had no need of a special explanation. The explanation was simply that he was a prophet. In this interpretation, the emphasis was not on the victim but on the murderers. Jesus' death revealed God's rejection of Israel for refusing conversion. This rejection of the prophet sent from God would be seen for all that it was when the prophet returned—as judge! His rejection, then, would mean perdition in the approaching judgment (Luke 12:8 and par.).

The primitive community now began to be persecuted for its missionary activity. Perhaps prison and death came into the picture. Now the followers of Jesus Christ began to share their leader's fate. Hence the logia: "Blest shall you be when men hate you . . . because of the Son of Man. . . . Thus it was that their fathers treated the prophets" (Luke 6:22–23).

There were words of those outside the fold, as well:

This is why the wisdom of God has said, "I will send them prophets and apostles, and some of these they will persecute and kill"; so that this generation will have to account for the blood of all the prophets shed since the foundation of the world. Their guilt stretches from the blood of Abel to the blood of Zechariah, who met his death between the altar and the sanctuary! Yes, I tell you, this generation will have to account for it [Luke 11:49–52].

Thus this community now not only interpreted Christ's death as the death of a prophet, but began to expect the following of Jesus Christ to involve Jesus' own fate.

A CRUCIFIED MESSIAH?

Other primitive Christian circles began very early to reflect on the meaning of Christ's death, especially from an apologetical viewpoint, both for the sake of those of the faith, and for purposes of responding to objections coming from the outside. In a faith context, the mighty theological challenge for the community was to find a place for Jesus in salvation history, and in the hopes of the only sacred scripture they possessed, the Old Testament. They had yearned for a glorious, triumphant messiah. The tortured victim on the cross was scarcely in the image of the messiah that the people and the apostles had expected. Was he who strove to deliver others from perdition not, in the end, lost himself? The cross seemed to militate against Jesus' messiahship. The suffering servant of Isaiah 53 had not yet been interpreted as referring to Jesus: no traditional exegesis would have supported such an interpretation. The suffering servant had always been interpreted as standing for the whole people of Israel, in exile among the gentiles. But he had never been understood as a figure of the messiah.

The internal difficulty was compounded by external circumstances. Other Jews were pointing to Deuteronomy 21:23, which pronounces a curse upon one who hangs on a tree, in order to give the lie to the claim being made by the Christians that Jesus was the messiah. The polemics must have been heated, as echoed in Galatians 3:13, where Paul solves the problem by reversing the terms: Christ had rendered *himself* accursed, in order to deliver us from the curse of our sins. His death on the tree, then, was evidence for, not against, his messiahship.

To demonstrate that the death of Jesus Christ on the cross was not absurd, the recounting of the event was always accompanied by references to scriptural passages. Paradoxical as the road trodden by Jesus Christ might seem to be, it was just as the scriptures had said it would be. It had been clearly marked out as the route of the will of God, and hence was charged with meaning and significance.

References to Christ's death were always accompanied by references to his resurrection. The intimation here was that Jesus' death was absurd, and contrary to messiahship, only apparently, only as seen from the outside. If you looked deeper, God had not abandoned Jesus. God had been with him in his suffering and death, and the resurrection showed that God was with him still. Jesus' resurrection revealed something that had lain hidden. What had seemed to be a scandal was now seen in the light of the resurrection. Now so many passages from the Old Testament suddenly became clear: they had been prophecies of Jesus' death and resurrection. Now everything was seen from God's viewpoint—Jesus' activity, his missionary enterprise, his death, his resurrection. God had been performing salvific action in Jesus at every step of the way—not only in his death, but in all that he had ever said, done, or undergone. God had been with Jesus at every turn, even in death. At last God's single, consistent plan is clear: to redeem humanity through Jesus Christ. The recalcitrance of other Jews cannot set this plan at naught. It can only "oblige" God—in the historico-salvific sense of the word "oblige"—to have the Son of God suffer. But that Son can suffer without betraying God and human beings. And then God intervenes to save him, snatching him from the jaws of death.

God does not directly will the death of Christ. God wills his fidelity to the end. This may mean Christ's death. And so the death of Christ is drawn within the historical framework where the ambiguous structure of good and evil prevails. From one point of view the death of Christ is an indictment of the wickedness of the persons who caused his death. But from another it is the symbol of a love stronger than death. In order to live this love to the very end, Jesus would not recoil from death itself. He accepted death as a burden that he could not escape. He accepted it in freedom. He accepted it as required of him by fidelity to his mission if he was to live that mission to the hilt.

It was in this perspective that the community composed the prophecies of the death and resurrection of Jesus Christ (Mark 8:31; 9:31; 10:33 and par.) and placed them on Jesus' lips. We cannot enter into a detailed analysis of these prophecies here. Suffice it to say that they are very probably of postpaschal origin. As we have seen, they represent a theological attempt to bestow meaning on the death of Christ in the light of God's plan. They are the product of an effort to assimilate Jesus' death into that plan. This is an easy matter now that the clarifying light of the resurrection has dawned. Furthermore, the prophecies of suffering have an eschatological aura about them. They foretell the death of the Son of Man. The death of Jesus Christ is an eschatological event, and thus is bound up with an eschatological judgment on the hardness of heart of the Jews outside the community and their idolatrous erection of the law into a way of salvation. The Son of Man, judged by human beings, paradoxically manifests himself as their judge.

THE DEATH OF CHRIST AS EXPIATION AND SACRIFICE

In many passages of the New Testament we encounter interpretations of Christ's death in a perspective of expiation, sacrifice, and redemption. It is in this matrix that we find the New Testament references to the expiatory sacrifice of the suffering servant of Yahweh (Isa. 52:13–53:12). Theology and piety alike have regarded this material as having been in Christ's consciousness from the start. Christ's death has generally been understood as a death that occurred for our sins and the expiation of the sin of the world. Today this is thought by many to be a major proof text of the Christian faith. But behind these faith formulations stands a slow, mighty, laborious theological endeavor.

The text of Isaiah 53 is clear enough:

> He was spurned and avoided by men,
>> a man of suffering, accustomed to infirmity,
> One of those from whom men hide their faces,
>> spurned, and we held him in no esteem.

> Yet it was our infirmities that he bore,
>> our sufferings that he endured,
> While we thought of him as stricken,
>> as one smitten by God and afflicted.
> But he was pierced for our offenses,
>> crushed for our sins;
> Upon him was the chastisement that makes us whole,
>> by his stripes we were healed. . . .
>> and smitten for the sin of his people. . . .

> If he gives his life as an offering for sin,
>> he shall see his descendants in a long life,
>> and the will of the Lord shall be accomplished through him. . . .
> Through his suffering, my servant shall justify many,
>> and their guilt he shall bear. . . .
> He surrendered himself to death
>> and was counted among the wicked;
> And he shall take away the sins of many,
>> and win pardon for their offenses [Isa. 53:3–12].

These words correspond so closely with the Christian community's conception of Christ's passion that they read like a prophecy of that passion. Had not everything written here been realized in Christ?

Was the community's perception objective? Did these early Christians uncover a latent, previously unrecognized, christological and messianic meaning in this passage from Second Isaiah?

These texts do constitute the first scriptural testimony to the expiatory, substitutive value of suffering and death. Probably in the intention of the sacred writer, however, they referred only to an Israel in exile, brought down to the depths of desolation as a people. This suffering is not in vain, the prophet is saying. Second Isaiah discerns a universal, vicarious significance in the suffering of Israel. No elaboration was developed in the later literature, however, and these passages were without any further influence on Old Testament theology. Nowhere in the Old Testament are these passages applied to the messiah. The figure here described bore no resemblance whatever to the expected messiah, who would surely be a victorious figure, indeed the ruler of the universe. The Isaian applications made to the messiah, especially in Ethiopian Henoch (esp. nos. 37-71), which dates from around the year 63 B.C., painted a picture of the messiah as he was in fact expected, and therefore included only three verses from Isaiah:

> See, my servant shall prosper
> he shall be raised high and greatly exalted. . . .
> So shall he startle many nations,
> because of him kings shall stand speechless;
> For those who have not been told shall see,
> those who have not heard shall ponder it
>   [Isa. 52:13-15].

Only these doxological passages were predicated of the messiah. The others, concerning his *kenosis* and humiliation, were *never* cited, and were even expurgated from the text (Kessler, *Bedeutung*, 29). We must surely say, then, that Isaiah 53 had no messianic connotation either before or during the time of Christ.

The primitive Christian community, however, as we have seen, applied Isaiah 53 to the passion and death of Jesus Christ. But this did not happen suddenly. Acts 8:32 and Mark 15:28, where Isaiah 53 is cited, are not among the earliest of the New Testament texts; nor, for that matter, does either of them cite the expiatory passages. In Acts 8:32, the eunuch is reading only this from Isaiah:

> Like a sheep he was led to the slaughter,
> like a lamb before its shearer he was silent
> and opened not his mouth.
> In his humiliation he was deprived of justice.
> Who will ever speak of his posterity,
> for he is deprived of his life on earth?
>   [Acts 8:32-33].

Mark 15:28 (omitted from many manuscripts [and from the NAB]) reads: "Thus the text of scripture came true that says, 'he was reckoned among criminals.' "

No reference is made to expiation or atonement in either text. This interpretation developed only at a later stage in the community's theological reflection.

Isaiah 53, then, was discovered only slowly by the Christian community. It is important to remember that it was not, at first, used to prove that the suffering Jesus was the messiah. There would simply have been no tradition to support such an argument. The rediscovery of Isaiah 53 did not arise out of meditation on the Isaian text itself. The process was a different one. Only at a later stage could Isaiah 53 be reread as a reference to values of satisfaction and atonement in Jesus' death.

Let us briefly observe how the first stage led into the second, in which Isaiah 53 acquired a messianic meaning of expiation and vicarious atonement.

A Fragment from a Hellenistic and Jewish-Christian Hymn: Romans 3:24–26a

At the heart of Paul's Letter to the Romans is a tradition that originated not with the original community, surely, but with a later community of Jewish converts. The tradition is liturgical, and probably had its *Sitz im Leben* (vital context) in a eucharistic liturgy:

> All men are now undeservedly justified by the gift of God, through the redemption wrought in Christ Jesus. Through his blood, God made him the means of expiation for all who believe. He did so to manifest his own justice, for the sake of remitting sins committed in the past—to manifest his justice in the present [Rom. 3:24–26a].

The formulation is clear: through his death (his "blood"), Christ became an expiatory sacrifice. Exegetes date this passage to approximately A.D. 40, in Antioch, Syria, where there was a Christian community of hellenized Jews of the diaspora.

It was in this particular Jewish atmosphere that another text was composed as well—one not received into the Jewish (or Christian) canon of scripture: the Fourth Book of Maccabees. This book recounts the bloody struggles of the Jews with King Antiochus IV Epiphanes under the leadership of the seven Maccabee brothers. A champion of Hellenism, Antiochus had sought to oblige the Jews to abandon their traditions and legal observances. Now he resorted to outright persecution, and many were the martyrs he made. We need only recall the aged Eleazar, or the seven Maccabees with their intrepid mother (4 Maccabees 5:1–17). These murders constituted a great problem for the Jews. Had these martyrs died in vain? What meaning had there been in the death of such innocents? They had not been personally guilty of anything deserving of death.

Yet they had died, and before their time. Then too: What meaning was there in the death of innocent children?

The Fourth Book of Maccabees seeks to give a satisfactory response to these questions. And its response is: the innocent victims of persecution have died not for any personal sin of their own. They have died in substitution for others. They have died in expiatory sacrifice for their whole people. Their premature death, even in the case of young children, has a meaning and a value: God accepts the death of these innocents in expiation for the sins of the people, and bestows pardon and forgiveness upon the people. In the seemingly absurd death of the innocent, the sacred writer saw God's salvific activity at work in the world. Their death had not really been absurd, then. It had had a function: the impetration of God's forgiveness.

God always wins in the end. Despite the sinfulness of persecutors, God does not permit the senselessness of their victims' death to abide. God transforms it into a vehicle of forgiveness—not of persecutors, surely, but of the sinful people (2 Macc. 6:28, 17:20–22, 18:4, 1:11).

This interpretation was developed outside Palestine, in the Judaism of the diaspora. In Palestine such a notion would simply never have occurred to anyone. Expiatory sacrifices offered in the temple—where animals were the victims, and gave up their blood—were all the expiation that was needed. The death, the blood, of a just human being would never have been regarded as an expiation for sin. Human blood had never been regarded as sacrificial, expiatory blood. The Jews of the diaspora, on the other hand, had no temple and no sacrifice. It was the most natural thing in the world, then, for them to think of innocent human blood as "sacrificial," or "expiatory," in a figurative, analogical sense.

Around the year 40—some ten years after Christ's death and resurrection—Jewish Christians of the diaspora, their religiosity bathed in this same theology, applied these representations to the death of Jesus. Further, let us notice, the *Sitz im Leben* of the Christian version of this theology seems to have been that of the eucharistic celebration. This is important. Not only was the death of Christ interpreted as a bloody expiation, but the association was made precisely in a context of the eucharistic celebration—precisely where the Lord's last supper, and his death, were commemorated as the inauguration of the new covenant. Now, this covenant could not help but suggest the covenantal sacrifice of Jeremiah 31:31–34, which in turn recalled Exodus 24:8: " 'This is the blood of the covenant which the Lord has made with you in accordance with all these words of his." And so the sacrificial, expiatory motif received even further reinforcement.

It was this motif of expiation and sacrifice of one's life for others, then, developed independently of any antecedent rereading of or meditation on Isaiah 53, that most probably permitted its consequent rereading by Christians in the sense of an expiatory, sacrificial meaning in the mystery of the death of Christ.

Eucharistic Texts and a Thematic of Sacrifice

The presence in the eucharistic texts of the motifs of sacrifice, expiation, and a covenant struck in the blood of Christ is too familiar to require any special demonstration. The verbal formula is clear: "This is my body which will be given up for you. . . . This is the cup of my blood, the blood of the new and everlasting covenant. It will be shed for you and for all."

Let us note that these words come to us in four versions: (1) 1 Corinthians 11:24; (2) Luke 22:19–20; (3) Mark 14:22–24; and (4) Matthew 26:26–28. (John 6:51–58 is the product of later reflection, around A.D. 100.)

But none of these four versions seems to have originated with the historical Jesus. To be sure, it is altogether certain that Christ celebrated a supper with his intimates. What he told them on that occasion, however, we cannot know for certain, and we have seen the reason why in the course of our foregoing analyses. The words of institution of the eucharist, as we have them today, originated at least ten years after the Last Supper and crucifixion. They reflect different eucharistic liturgies as these were celebrated in the various communities—those of Luke and Paul in one group, and those of Mark and Matthew in another.

In Judaic circles where the death of the just one was already interpreted as expiation and vicarious atonement in behalf of the whole people, and thus also in the circle of those who understood the new covenant of Jesus, ratified by his death, as an expiatory sacrifice, a new association was now created. This new perception made way for the ascription of a new and different meaning to the death of the Lord. Now his death found its place in the long line of martyrdoms for the faith—the redemptive, expiatory, sacrificial deaths of the innocents. Now the death of Christ was seen as an act of impetration for forgiveness of sin. It had inaugurated a new covenant between God and the people of God, the church.

In this light, the meaning of the eucharistic formula, "This is my body which will be given up for you . . . this is the cup of my blood, the blood of the new and everlasting covenant; it will be shed for you and for all," becomes clear. It is the expression of the great "constant" in all of Jesus' life: that of being-for-others. Jesus gave himself continually. In him God was present "salvifically," in the fullness of elevating grace, in the fullness of a freedom that builds, that constructs. Jesus lived an intimacy with the lost, outcast children of God such that he could not only signify, but actually be the vehicle of, God's forgiveness. However, the Last Supper speaks to us not so much of Christ's earthly life, where this attitude of his in favor of human beings was actually manifested, but rather of his life from the moment of his death—from the moment, then, of the crisis that his life of love provoked, as it proceeded slowly but surely toward its liquidation (see John 12). Just as his life, so also his death was a continuous bestowal of self—truly a sacrifice for others.

By way of these theological associations, then, with the help of the Books of

Maccabees and Isaiah 53 alike, Christians could now say: through Christ's expiatory death, God forgives the sin of humankind, removes the obstacles to salvation, and approaches human creatures in a salvific manner, establishing a new covenant in Christ's blood. In Jesus' earthly activity, God, the bountiful and merciful Lord of creation, had drawn near human creatures, seeking to found a new community (covenant) with them: with Zacchaeus, with the Samaritan at the well, with the tax collectors, with every human being. And Jesus ratified this attitude in his death.

The bloody-sacrifice model as an articulation of God's redemption in Christ is inadequate as an expression of the whole of God's salvific activity. That activity extends all through Christ's life, encompassing all that Christ did. I repeat what I have said so often: it is not only Christ's death, but his whole life, that is redemptive.

The three soteriological models that we have now examined reveal the breadth and depth of the reflection undertaken by the primitive communities in their effort to unveil the transcendent meaning implicit in the death of Christ. As we see, this meaning did not strike the early Christians like a bolt from the blue. It came to them gradually, under the influence of the Holy Spirit. God's revelation does not obviate human effort. It requires that effort. It enables it, and guides it in a particular direction.

Saint Paul will make still further strides toward a more complete grasp of the salvific, liberative aspect of the death of Jesus Christ. Let us examine some of his contributions. We shall see that Paul, too, has things to say that will be most enlightening for our own problematic.

THE DEATH OF CHRIST IN THE THEOLOGICAL REFLECTIONS OF SAINT PAUL

In the first phase of his work, Paul's all-pervasive concern is the resurrection. We need only read his two early letters to the Thessalonians, written in the year 49, some twenty years after his conversion. Christ's resurrection has stirred a hope of resurrection for all. Surely we are on the threshold of the new age. In a voice ringing with apocalypticism, Paul speaks of the imminent coming of the Lord (1 Thess. 4:15-17). His enthusiasm knows no bounds. The second coming of Christ has given him new hope, new reason to live. Triumphant paradoxes abound. The Spirit, the presence of the risen one in the world, has replaced the law in this fleeting interim before the Lord's coming. No one is any longer under any constraint but that of the Spirit. The important thing is to be patient a little longer, to hope with a white-hot hope, to abandon any concern for the things of this world, or the legalistic, pious observance of its order—for this will presently be swallowed up in Christ's victory.

In a second phase, however, the Pauline theology veers off in another direction. The new departure begins with First and Second Corinthians. "I determined that while I was with you I would speak of nothing but Jesus Christ and him crucified" (1 Cor. 2:2), writes the apostle. He had begun his letter with: "We preach Christ crucified—a stumbling block to Jews, and an absurdity to Gentiles; but to those who are called, Jews and Greeks alike, Christ the power of God and the wisdom of God" (1 Cor. 1:23–24).

Why this shift in direction? To be sure, the resurrection thematic has not simply disappeared from Paul's letters. The core of Pauline theology will always be the resurrection of Jesus Christ. After all, the risen Christ is the only Jesus Paul has ever known. The epitome of Paul's theological message is the latent meaning for the world in the resurrection of Christ. He carries the implications of the resurrection to its ultimate consequences, whether for the past, so that Judaism must be abandoned, or for the future, with its new human being, its new heaven and new earth. Whenever Paul speaks of Christ's death, he sets it in correlation with his resurrection. There is someone who was dead but who has been raised up, and lives.

But now concrete problems in the communities threaten precisely the theological content of the resurrection. The resurrection motif has been turned into an opium, has become the hotbed of an enthusiasm that is perverting life, inverting all norms for living. Paul encounters enemies in the community. They falsify the good news of the resurrection. Their conceptions allow no room for the cross, with its whole mystique of *kenosis*, humility, and asceticism for its followers.

Add to this that for Roman citizens and Greek converts this new cult of a crucified criminal was an out-and-out scandal. Suppose, in our own day, someone were to venerate or worship a person who had died in the electric chair for some heinous offense. And so now there was a group of Christians who wanted to ignore, or even reject, any theology of spirituality of Jesus' cross.

Paul, then, sees himself obliged to develop a theology of the cross. This new theology will spring from an altogether concrete situation: altercations in the community. Had it not been for these problems, perhaps Paul would never have erected the problematic of the cross into a theological theme. It is not, then, a theme in itself. The main theme of Christianity continues to be the resurrection. It is the resurrection that has bathed the world in newness of life. But the resurrection stands against a backdrop of death, and it is only against this backdrop that it makes any sense to talk about resurrection. Otherwise we should be right back in Greek mythology. There would be nothing new. Sooner or later, then, theology was going to have to deal with the cross. But in the concrete, this development was due to certain distortions arising in the communities of Corinth. The meaning Paul ascribes to Christ's death appears in his confrontation with his enemies.

Let us examine this new theology of Paul's in its polemical context. The letters of Paul, with the possible exception of the Letter to the Romans, are occasional pieces. That is, they are closely bound up with the concrete problematic of a given situation. Paul's is an "engaged" theology, and does not show a great deal of systematization. It is functional. This does not mean that it has no systematic thought behind it. Paul was a theologian of extraordinary acumen. However, he never developed a systematic synthesis, and it is only his various situational interventions that afford us a glimpse of the extraordinary architecture of his theological edifice.

Not Freedom from Others, but Freedom for Others

In his First Letter to the Corinthians, Paul writes against certain self-styled theologians who have been converted to the faith by his preaching but who have distorted his theological intuitions. They have denied that there will be a resurrection for the followers of Christ. We have already been raised up, they declare, and they represent their reception of the Spirit in baptism (1 Cor. 6:11) as resurrection from the dead. They are "pneumatic" now (1 Cor. 2:13–16; 3:1; 12:1; 14:37). They document their possession of the Spirit of resurrection with spiritual charisms, with the gift of wisdom (1 Cor. 1:20; 2:1; 4–13; 12:8), glossolalia, and ecstasy (1 Cor. 12:10; 13:1; 14:2–5). The "charismatics" are puffed up with vain glory. They are almost fanatically enthusiastic. They are known as "psychics"—spiritual, "pneumatic" persons (1 Cor. 2:14), and they contrast themselves with "carnal" or immature persons (1 Cor. 3:3; 13:11).

These self-styled spiritual individuals imagined that they were already living the fullness of resurrection. They were already wise (1 Cor. 1:26; 3:18; 6:5), they flaunted their charismata, they looked down on those whom they judged less spiritual, or "carnal" (1 Cor. 8:1, 10; 13:2, 8). They esteemed themselves the perfect ones (1 Cor. 2:6; 13:10; 14:20). They refused to believe in a future resurrection, then, because the resurrection had already occurred (1 Cor. 15:12; cf. 2 Tim. 2:18). Accordingly, they had no interest in the earthly Jesus, Jesus crucified. Their concern was only with the risen Jesus. Indeed they cursed the fleshly Jesus (1 Cor. 12:3).

Paul himself, in another context, was to say that the Jesus *kata sarka*, "according to the flesh," held little interest for him—that his concern was with Jesus *kata Pneuma*, the Jesus according to the Spirit (2 Cor. 5:6). But this attitude had degenerated into an ideology of self-seeking and status.

In the name of a resurrection that had already occurred, Paul's adversaries called for a libertine freedom (1 Cor. 9:1, 19; 10:29; cf. 7:21–22). Everything was permitted (1 Cor. 6:12; 10:23). Morality was a thing of the past. A man could visit prostitutes or sleep with his mother, as he pleased (1 Cor. 6:13–18). Christians could participate in pagan sacrifices (1 Cor. 8:1–6; 10:23–30). The Jesus who had walked the earth, Jesus weak and crucified, was ignored.

What Paul proclaimed for the near future, these converted Hellenists transferred to the present. Theirs was a completely "realized eschatology," theirs the psychic enthusiasm of a plenitude and perfection already attained in the here and now.

Paul responds with a devastating argument. Point by point he refutes his adversaries, in light of a theology of the cross and Christ crucified: *Christos stauromenos*. The cross denounces all this boasting. The cross rips the mask from the face of all this selfish power and pharisaical perfection. The cross shows the "goodness" of the world for what it is: insanity and manure. If the world had power to save, if the wisdom of the Greeks could redeem, if the Judaic law with all its wondrous portents could set us free, then of course the cross would be unnecessary. The cross would have no place at all. But as it is, the cross shows the flimsiness of all Greek wisdom and all Judaic holiness. The cross is madness, yes, and the cross is scandal. Yet it is the only wisdom. Greek and Jewish wisdom are so many lies. They lead only up blind alleys. See where they have led in the community! Values are set topsy-turvy, amorality reigns, one group exalts itself over another. Baptism creates a community with the Lord (1 Cor. 1:9): the Spirit we receive in baptism is not a spirit of division, but of union (1 Cor. 12). Charisms are not for self-aggrandizement; they are for the edification, the upbuilding, of the community. Paul would rather speak one word that others can understand than ten thousand that no one understands. Communion with Christ is a radical impediment to taking up with prostitutes (1 Cor. 6:12–20).

And so Paul dispels the enthusiasts' illusions with the wisdom of the cross, confronting them with the concrete realities of the present, where flesh and blood prevail. As long as these prevail, there can be no present reign of God. God's reign is already present with baptism, faith, the eucharist, the *Pneuma*, yes. But the flesh exists, too, with its works. The cross shows what flesh can do. Flesh can cripple, flesh can kill. Christ was done to death by the work of the flesh. The Christian must live an ascetical dimension, then. Hope in the resurrection is not today's transport to the world of tomorrow. Paul knows that he must live his hope where he is—in the old world, where sin prevails. Hence the need for prudence, hence the imperative of a humble following of the cross, hence the urgency of renunciation, care for others and love for others, be they weak or strong. It is this experience of the cross that is the power and wisdom of God (1 Cor. 1:24).

The cross of Christ has become the criterion of Christian wisdom. In Christian wisdom is the love that endures everything, forgives everything, believes in everything, hopes for everything, excuses everything. This wisdom, this love, is anything but boasting, pridefulness, or proneness to anger and resentment. It is patient, kind, and happy to see truth prevail (1 Cor. 13:4–6). The cross is the measure of Christian truth. It is also the measure of the Christian's concrete behavior. In the cross is the discernment of spirits and practices.

The cross acquires an eschatologico-critical function. The cross cannot be leapt over, or emptied (1 Cor. 1:17; cf. 12:3). It cannot be regarded as out-moded, a thing of the past (Gal. 5:11). It cannot be heroicized, and regarded as some mighty, once-and-for-all deed of a bygone time (2 Cor.).

The cross obliges us to accept a different sort of wisdom, God's wisdom, which is found not in lofty words, but in everyday activities, and everyday weakness. Those who, like the enthusiasts of Corinth, sneer at the weak, at those still walking the road of the Spirit, may as well sneer at the crucified Jesus himself, as well, and curse him. And indeed they do. But they forget that it was in weakness that God has revealed power and salvation. Because Jesus, the lord of the world, was weak, he made a commitment to others. He gave his life for them, and so snatched them from isolation and abandonment. He walked the path not for freedom *from* others, but of freedom *for* others, and he walked it to the end. He walked it consistently, never faltering. In his weakness, the weakness of one altogether powerless, is manifested the might of love itself, the power to conquer hearts, the strength to initiate a genuine salvific revolution. Death and the cross hurl their challenge: Come, follow! Without the cross, the reality of the resurrection would be empty of all meaning. Paul must defend the cross, then. The cross is part and parcel of Christian faith.

Soteriological and Eschatological Function of Jesus' Death

The Second Letter to the Corinthians paints another picture. Between the writing of the First and Second Corinthians, something else has happened. Wonder-working preachers have appeared in the community, pneumatics in the Greek style, known as *theioi andres*, "divine men," claiming letters of recommendation from Paul (1 Cor. 3:1; 5:12; 10:12). Like the "spiritual" individuals of the first letter, these newcomers, too, are enthusiasts for the novelty of the Spirit. They claim that the risen Jesus speaks in them with miraculous signs (2 Cor. 12:11–21; 13:3). But they too have difficulties admitting the value of Christ's death and cross. That was all a symbol of weakness, they say—scarcely a sign of the presence of the Spirit. Paul himself, who seemed weak to them with his pedestrian oratorical style, was regarded as without signs of legitimation on the part of the Spirit and the risen Jesus (1 Cor. 1:17; 2:1–5; 4:8–13; 15:8–11; 2 Cor. 11:21; 10:1, 10; 11:6).

By way of contrast with the "spiritual" individuals of the first letter, this new group has great respect for Christ. Christ has not only brought a new covenant, but has fulfilled the covenant of Moses through his miraculous portents. He was a *theios aner*, a divine man, a hero in the Greek style. He was a superman, bursting the frontiers of the human and entering the sphere of the divine. He has documented his greatness, his grandeur, with marvelous deeds, and thereby become indeed the manifestation of God (2 Cor. 13:3; 12:9).

Clearly there is no room for the cross and suffering in this image of Christ. Over against this concept of Jesus' magnificence and glorification, Paul sets the cross and suffering, weakness and death. Thereby he seeks to rescue the Christian mystery from Greek mythology—from the reduction of Christ to the heroism of Greek popular culture. Christ's resurrection would have been only an exaltation, a miraculous portent. It would not have been a transfiguration of death and the cross.

And so Paul insists that Christ lived the earthly conditions of life, and that he died *in conspectu omnium* (2 Cor. 5:14). The exceptional thing about Jesus Christ was this: that in his weakness and death God had posited the salvation of all humankind definitively and totally. In his poverty Christ bestowed on us God's wealth (2 Cor. 8:9). In his helplessness he communicated to us the power of God's life (2 Cor. 13:4); in his life he made himself small, and delivered himself for us (2 Cor. 5:14). Thereby he brought us salvation and divine reconciliation.

Reconciliation, new life, and salvation happen whenever this way of existing and living, Jesus Christ's way, is imitated and lived by human beings (2 Cor. 6:10; 12:9–10; 5:18–20).

Paul demolished the illusion, which had gained currency in the community, that our present situation can be perfected to the point where it will actually be self-redeeming. Christ, for Paul, is no Greek hero vaunting his Herculean strength, his Apollonian intelligence, his preternatural thaumaturgy. Christ, with his death and his cross, is the crisis, in the original sense of the word, of all human undertakings: their judgment, their moment of truth. They all come to an end on the cross. Christ's resurrection cannot, then, be understood as a sublimation of the present human situation. It has meaning only if human beings die. Then, and only then, can they be re-assumed and fulfilled, not by their own efforts and doing, not by their own creation, but by God.

Thus the resurrection of Jesus Christ marks a quantum leap in history. God's eschatological intervention consists in this resurrection. The old has passed away (2 Cor. 5:17): those who live as Christ lived, and who therefore are in Christ—those who have accepted death and the cross, then—are new creatures, raised up. This newness of life is already present, yes, but not completely, for we still suffer and grieve (2 Cor. 6:4–10). Here is the foundation of hope and trust in the God who raises the dead to life (2 Cor. 1:9). Salvation and the world of tomorrow exist only for those who open themselves to the love of God made manifest in the weakness of the cross, to those who accept their own weakness. Jesus did not build his greatness at others' cost. He made himself small in order to serve others, and he served them to the end, for he died for them all (2 Cor. 5:14; Gal. 2:20; Rom. 8:35).

In the cross, then, Paul finds the argument he needs to combat both the enthusiasm of Corinth's Hellenists, and the evolutionism of its hellenized Judeo-Christians.

Death of Christ: Deliverance from the Curse of the Law

In his Letter to the Galatians, Paul counters the move of a group of Christians who insisted on maintaining Jewish traditions side by side with the novelty of Christianity. The issue was the observance of the Mosaic law, which was presumed to render persons just before God. Paul had been a Pharisee. He had experienced what it meant to live under the law, and now he mounted a vigorous theological campaign against the legalistic contamination of Christianity. Make your salvation dependent on the observance of the law and you are lost. You will never be able to be sure you have observed the whole law perfectly. You will always have left something out, you will always owe something, and so you will always be under the power of sin and the curse it merits (Gal. 3:22–23; 4:3; 2:17; 3:10).

But God has delivered us from this curse, precisely by having Jesus be born under the sign of sin and curse (Gal. 4:4; 3:13). Jesus became curse that we might be blessing. It is not our works that will save us. These always fall short of the demands of the law. What saves us is faith in Jesus Christ, who took our situation on himself and saved us (Gal. 5:1). In God, and not in our works, we have our security. Not that faith dispenses from works. Works follow upon faith. They are the consequence of faith, and of trusting surrender to God, who, in Jesus Christ, has accepted us and freed us. And so Paul insists that we are justified by faith in Jesus Christ, without the works of the Law (Gal. 2:16).

This faith in God through Jesus Christ truly frees us for the real work of the world. We need no longer accumulate works of piety in order to be saved. They will not do the job. But if we are saved by faith, then we can bend our efforts toward love for others, toward the building of a more loving community of sisters and brothers in this world, in the power of the faith and the salvation with which we appear in God's sight. And so Paul says that the freedom for which we have been liberated (Gal. 5:1) ought to lead us not to anarchy, but to the service of others (Gal. 5:13), ought to lead us to perform good works, the works of communion, joy, and mercy (Gal. 5:6).

In his death, Christ delivered us from a neurotic obsession with storing up "good works," pious deeds, for the salvation of our soul. These only tie our hands. They make us only pharisaically religious. Free at last, we can use our hands for the service of love. Christianity introduces a new dimension here. It liberates the human being for building the world, not for practicing a piety of mere worship whose purpose is to save one's own soul. Piety, prayer, and religion are manifestations of a love of God already received, a salvation already communicated. Their structure is that of thanksgiving and freedom from concern.

Paul developed and preached a good many other approaches to Christ's death, as well, especially in his whole thematic of justification. We cannot enter into all of these approaches here. Let us dwell only on certain elements that hold some promise of shedding light on the theological moment in which we live today.

LETTER TO THE HEBREWS: CHRIST'S DEATH AS SACRIFICE

The Letter to the Hebrews is one of the greatest theological discourses of the New Testament. It is certainly from the hand of a disciple of Paul. The time is one of persecution (Heb. 10:32–36; 13:2). The community is discouraged and without hope (Heb. 5:11–14; 2:15; 12:12–13). It knows the truth of what Cicero said of the cross: that it is a *crudelissimum taeterrimumque supplicium*, an incredibly cruel and humiliating torture (*Against Verres*, book 2, chapter 5, no. 165). What a shameful death Christ died (Heb. 12:2; 13:13)! Many of the community had apostatized (Heb. 10:39; 12:15). The shepherd of the flock known as "the Hebrews" writes a letter of encouragement, then, to strengthen and console that flock. He uses a twofold argument:

1. Believing means suffering and dying, too, as the gateway to the heavenly plenitude (Heb. 12). This is Jesus Christ's view of matters. After all, Jesus Christ suffered, was tortured, and had to learn the painful lesson of obedience and the acceptance of a sorrowful death. He is the example and prototype of faith and fidelity (Heb. 12:3). He is the one who runs before us on our journey to our heavenly country.

2. With Jesus, final salvation has appeared for us all. By way of explanation the author appeals to the great Jewish Day of Atonement. Through his own blood, not through the blood of sacrifices, High Priest Jesus has entered once and for all into the Holy of Holies, crossing beyond the veil (the veil of death). Now he stands before the face of God, making expiation for us and interceding for us (Heb. 7:25; 9:24; cf. 8:1ff.; 9:12; 10:14). Death itself is resplendent in the light of this "temple worship." Christ is sacrifice, victim, and priest, all at once.

However, one must be careful here. Christ's sacrificial death is different from the temple sacrifices. And so the argument begins: God does not wish sacrifices and offerings. They are not pleasing to God. God gave Christ a body to do God's will (Heb. 10:5-7). God has rejected sacrifices. God has initiated a new discipline to replace it. Christ is the end of all ritual sacrifices. Nor indeed may he himself be understood as a ritual sacrifice. Here we need only read:

> Through him let us continually offer God a sacrifice of praise, that is, the fruit of lips which acknowledge his name. Do not neglect good deeds and generosity; God is pleased by sacrifices of that kind [Heb. 13:15].

We see how faith has liberated human beings for liberative, "secular," activity in the world.

In this interpretation, Christ is the sole expiation for the sins of the world, and he is still exercising his function, still interceding with God. His sacrifice is not confined to the moment of his death. Thus his death does not constitute a salvific act, properly speaking. It makes that act possible, however, because it was through his death that this high priest entered the Holy of Holies to inaugurate his activity of intercession. Jesus Christ has not become a priest in time, according to the order of Aaron, but a priest beyond time, in eternity, according to the order of Melchizedech (Heb. 7:11-28). His is a transhistorical, eschatological priesthood, in the dispensation of resurrection. It is in this sense that Christ continues his ministry of intercession and redemption forevermore.

Though Son, Christ was willing to suffer because he willed to be high priest permanently, for humankind. His sacrifice cannot be identified with the Mass. The sacred writer had no specific ritual act, not even the eucharist, in mind. He is speaking only of the salvific meaning of Christ's presence at the right hand of God through his death. It was his death that permitted Christ to be high priest. This is the function he is now performing, and it is in virtue of this function that we are given help, and are permanently redeemed.

Chapter 7

Main Interpretations
of Christ's Death
in Theological Tradition:
Validities and Invalidities

Now that we have considered how Jesus interpreted his death, and then how the primitive church interpreted it, let us examine the principal images utilized by our faith tradition to invest the salvific death of Jesus Christ with intelligibility, significance, and currency.

These images may appear very different from one another. But they all seek to convey a single, profound faith and hope: thanks to God, we have been liberated by our Lord Jesus Christ (Rom. 7:24-25).

How may such a rich, suggestive datum of faith be made credible and acceptable? Do the images used in piety, liturgy, and theology to express Jesus Christ's liberation really succeed in setting in relief the genuinely liberative aspect of Christ's life, death, and resurrection? Or do they rather conceal this aspect? We say: Christ redeemed us by his precious blood—he expiated, made satisfaction for, our sins by his death, offering up his own life as a sacrifice for the redemption of all. What does all this really mean? Do we understand what we are saying? Can we really think that God had grown angry, and that Christ's death appeased God? Can someone replace another and die for his or her sins, die in that person's stead, while the beneficiary continues to sin? Who should change—God, from angry to benign, or men and women, from sinners to just? We profess: Christ delivered us from sin! And we keep on sinning. He delivered us from death! And we keep on dying. He reconciled us with God! And we keep on making ourselves God's enemies. What concrete, genuine meaning is there in this liberation from death, sin, and enmity?

The vocabulary employed to express Jesus Christ's liberation translates social situations. It conveys ideological interests, as well. It articulates the cultural tendencies of a given age. A heavily juridical mentality will speak in juridical, commercial terms of redemption, using language like "redeeming Satan's rights of dominion over the sinner." We shall hear of satisfaction, merit, penal substitution, and the like. A ritualistic mentality will express itself in terms of sacrifice. A third mind-set, focusing on the social and cultural relevance of human liberation, will preach the liberation bestowed by Jesus Christ. What do we really mean when we say that the death of Christ was part of the Father's salvific plan? Is Jesus' rejection by the religious authorities, or Judas's betrayal, or the Roman death sentence part of this plan? But these persons were not puppets in an a priori plan, a suprahistorical drama. They were concrete agents, responsible for their own decisions. Christ's death, as we have seen, was a human death: the consequence of a concrete, particular life. Christ's death was by capital punishment, in retribution for the particular, historical attitudes he had assumed.

A fetishistic repetition of old sacred formulas will not be enough. We must seek to understand these formulas, try to capture the reality that they attempt to convey. Now, this salvific reality can and should be expressed in many ways. This was true in the past, and this should be true in the present. Today we speak of liberation. We use this expression to convey a certain directioning, a certain incarnation, of our faith. Saint Anselm did no more when he expressed himself in terms of vicarious satisfaction. Without consciously adverting to it, perhaps, he was translating a mind-set proper to his own particular, medieval world, in which an offense against the highest sovereign could not be repaired by an inferior vassal. For our part, we seek to embody our own insight, our own perception, which focuses on the socio-structural dimension of human captivity and alienation. How is Christ a liberator from this antireality *as well*?

The primary intent of the questions that I shall be asking here will be to dismantle, to tear down. I propose to subject to critical analysis three common representations of Christ's salvific action—those of sacrifice, redemption, and satisfaction—and criticize them. I shall not be concerned with construction. The three models, the three theological constructs, that I shall examine here are calculated to yield, in the context of a determinate cultural time and space, an understanding of the salvific meaning of Jesus Christ. When I say I intend to dismantle them, I mean that I propose (1) to examine the blueprint for the particular "edifice," the particular model, under consideration, (2) to follow the construction process, step by step, with particular attention to any "dated" material, especially if any of that material is intrinsically inappropriate, and finally (3) to isolate the permanent validity of the meaning and intent of the particular model. Surely I need make no apologies for the legitimacy of a critical approach. Criticism simply means discernment of the value, scope, and limitations of a given proposition.

WHAT IN JESUS CHRIST IS PROPERLY REDEMPTIVE: THE BEGINNING (THE INCARNATION) OR THE END (THE CROSS)?

We may note in theological tradition, as well as in official liturgical texts still prescribed for worship, a certain confinement in their conceptions of redemption in the concrete. This tradition, and these texts, concentrate redemption at one of two antipodal points. They focus exclusively either on the beginning of Christ's life, the incarnation, or on the end of that life, the passion and cross. Even the ancient creeds adopt this abstract way of viewing redemption, moving directly from Jesus' incarnation to his death and resurrection, omitting his earthly life—the salvific value of all his words, attitudes, actions, and reactions.

The Greek Approach

A theology under the thumb of a Greek mentality will posit the decisive point of redemption in the incarnation of God. According to classic Greek metaphysics, God is synonymous with life, perfection, and immortality: creation, then, because it is not God, is necessarily corruptible, imperfect, and mortal. This is an ineluctable consequence of the ontological structure of created being. It makes room for fatality, not sin. Redemption means the elevation of the world to the sphere of the divine. Thus the human being, together with the entire cosmos, is divinized. Both are delivered from the weight of their own internal limitations. Saint Athanasius's concise statement in *De Incarnatione Verbi* is arresting: "God became human so that humans might become God" (chap. 54). Redemption enters the world through the incarnation. In Jesus Christ, the deathless, infinite God encounters the mortal, finite creature, and it is the latter that must yield. This antipodal point alone, then, that of the incarnation, is enough to touch and redeem all creation. There is relatively little interest in the concrete human being Jesus of Nazareth, his personal journey through life, the conflict he provoked with the religious and political authorities of his time. All interest is concentrated on the universal humanity represented by Jesus Christ. God is the agent of redemption. It is God's self-communication that elevates and divinizes creation. This model of redemption abstracts from the historical element in Jesus of Nazareth. The incarnation is understood statically: it is understood as the first moment of the virginal conception of Jesus the "God-Man." Nothing else matters. Left out of account is the dynamic, historical aspect of Christ's growth to maturity, his words, the various phases of his life, his decisions, his temptations, his encounters. Are not all of these immediately assumed by God the moment that they occur?

In this conceptualization, redemption bestowed today is independent of concrete human historicity. There is no thought of the expression of redemption in a transformed praxis of greater justice and equity among brothers and sisters. Attention is riveted instead on a subjective participation in an objective event that took place in the past and is rendered present today by the church, as the prolongation of the incarnation of the Word, through sacraments and worship, which now effectuate the divinization of human beings.

The Roman Approach

A heavily ethico-juridical theology, in the spirit of ancient Rome, will locate the decisive moment of our redemption in Christ's passion and death. For

Roman thought, the world is imperfect not so much by virtue of its ontological makeup as creaturely, but owing to the presence of sin and the abuse of human freedom. The human being has offended God, transgressing the right order of nature; therefore the human being must repair this wrong; hence the need for merit, sacrifice, conversion, reconciliation. Only thus will the pristine order be reestablished, and the tranquility of order prevail.

And so God takes the initiative, condescending to send to human beings his own Son to make vicarious satisfaction, by his death, for the infinite offense committed by the human being. Christ came to die and make reparation. Jesus' incarnation and life have value only insofar as they prepare for and anticipate his death. Here the central figure is not really God, but the human Jesus, who by means of his death satisfies for the evil perpetrated. There is nothing radically new, such as divinization. It is a matter of restoring a primitive order of justice and holiness.

INADEQUACIES OF THESE IMAGES OF THE REDEMPTION

Both of these models are schizophrenic. Both tear the incarnation away from the passion. One model concentrates redemption in Christ's incarnation. The other reduces it to his death. The concrete life of Jesus of Nazareth is drained of all meaning, and redemption becomes singularly abstract. Was not Jesus' whole life equally liberative? Did he not demonstrate the nature of redemption in his manner of life, in the way he behaved in various situations, in his attitude in the face of death? We find none of this, however, in either of these abstract models, the incarnational or the staurological (from *stauros*, "cross").

Beginning and end are posited as independent, self-subsisting quantities. No relationship obtains between them. That relationship, of course, is the concrete life of Jesus of Nazareth. His death on the cross was not a metaphysical necessity, it was the consequence of a conflict, and the terminal point of a juridical process. It was therefore a decision taken in the exercise of human freedom.

Both conceptions, furthermore, situate redemption in the past. Redemption enjoys no relationship with mediations of the present. There is no room for asking how liberation from social sin, redemption from structural injustices, or a struggle against hunger and human misery are to be identified in any way with Jesus Christ's redemption. Neither model admits of any consistent response to these burning theological questions.

We shall not discover the real nature of redemption and liberation through Jesus Christ in abstract, formal models that shred the unity of the life of Jesus Christ—the concrete unity of the actual, historical path trodden by Jesus of Nazareth in his life, his activity, his demands, in the conflicts he stirred up, and in his death and resurrection. Redemption is basically a praxis, a historical process, verified (in the etymological sense of the word: "rendered true") in the turbulent reality of a concrete situation. Jesus inaugurated his redemption with the new praxis he demanded and introduced into the world he found.

The incarnation also implies God's entry into a world marked by a particular religion and a particular culture, and God's transformation of that world. Nor does God assume that world is all peace and tranquility, serenely sacralizing all that God encounters. God took up that concrete world critically, purifying it, demanding conversion, change, reorientation, and liberation.

It is not my intent to ignore the ontological implications of the redemptive road trodden by Jesus Christ. Why is it that none other than he has managed the liberation of women and men? Why has he alone had the energy, the vitality, to live his life in such a perfect, transparent way, to live a life so divine and so human, that it has meant redemption—that it has signified the genuine life that has ever been the object of the human quest? He accomplished all of this not because he was a genius of humanism and piety, or simply because of the merit of his commitment to his task, but because God was incarnate in him—because *God became present* in him, as deliverance and reconciliation of the world. This ontological proposition, however, is verified only as the ultimate explanation of the concrete history lived, undergone, suffered, and surmounted by Jesus of Nazareth as the Gospels depict him. In this life that included everything—even death and resurrection— salvation and redemption have shone forth—not abstractly, not in antipodal points, and not in formulations, but in deeds and actions, in the consistent oneness of a life of total self-gift to others and to God. The magnificence of this gift of self in its various implications has already been considered above.

A Third Approach

The inadequacy of a faith-inspired understanding of Christ's liberative activity can appear in other ways as well. An inadequacy in its starting point will not be the only lethal flaw in this understanding. A limitation of the act of redemption to the incarnation or to the cross is only one way to vitiate an adequate expression of the redemption wrought by Jesus Christ. There is also the problem of the articulation of the images employed to express and communicate the universal, definitive value of his salvific activity. Here I am thinking of three current models in theology and piety: the images of expiatory sacrifice, redemption in the sense of ransom, and vicarious satisfaction.

These three models rest on a common pedestal: sin, triply interpreted. Sin as an offense against God is an offense calling for condign reparation and satisfaction. Sin as committed by human beings demands the punishment of the culprit in a sacrifice of expiation. Finally, sin as it affects the relationship between human beings and God signifies a breach, an enslavement of the human being delivered over to the dominion of Satan, and requires redemption in the sense of ransom.

In all three of these ways of understanding the salvation brought by Jesus

Christ, human beings are helpless to satisfy an outraged divine justice. And so they abide in injustice. Liberation consists precisely in Jesus Christ's substitution for human beings—Jesus Christ's effectuation of what human beings ought to have done in terms of satisfaction and had been unable to do. The divine mercy, according to this theology, is manifested in the Father's dispatch of his Son, in place of sinful creatures, to make full satisfaction to the divine justice of an offended God. The Son will now receive the wages of sin, which are death, thereby pay the ransom due to Satan, and so deliver humankind from condemnation. All of this is effectuated by the expiatory, satisfactory, redemptive death of Jesus Christ. Who willed the death of Christ? This theology will answer: the Father, as the way to expiate sin and reinstate an order of justice that had been violated.

Here, obviously, the thinking that prevails is a juridical, formal attitude toward sin, justice, and the relationship between God and human beings. The concepts of expiation, reparation, satisfaction, ransom, and merit conceal rather than communicate the rich novelty of the liberation that comes to us in Jesus Christ. The historical element of Jesus' life is forcibly suppressed. Jesus' death is not seen as a consequence of his life. It is seen as a predetermined phenomenon, occurring independently of human decisions like Jesus' rejection by the religious authorities, his betrayal by Judas, or Pilate's sentence. Can God, our Father, find joy and satisfaction in the violent, bloody death of the cross?

We must dismantle these images, take them apart, in order to safeguard, in our thinking inspired by faith, the authentically liberative element in the life, death, and resurrection of Jesus Christ. Nowhere in the soteriology before us do we hear anything of Jesus' resurrection. Christ need not have been resurrected. It is enough to have suffered, to have spilled his blood, to have died on the cross, in order to have accomplished his deed of redemption. We cannot ignore the grave limitations of this approach to an interpretation of the salvific meaning of Jesus Christ.

Furthermore, these three models have an aura of the archaic, the mythological, about them. As such, they compromise the historical, factual content of Jesus Christ's liberation. What do we mean when we say that Christ's death was vicarious? Can someone die in another's stead, without that other's freely given authorization and delegation? Then how are we to conceptualize this vicarious mediation on the part of Jesus Christ in the case of men and women who lived before him or after him, or who have never heard of the gospel or redemption? Will redemption be accomplished by the suffering and death—punishment—undergone by this innocent person, who is free of fault, who is without any criminal guilt that would merit this punishment, this suffering, and death? What framework would lend any intelligibility to the concept of a universal vicarious character attaching to the deed of Jesus Christ? What experience would make it possible for us to comprehend, accept, and believe in Christ's salvific, liberative mediation in behalf of all humankind in terms of a vicarious death? These questions cannot be left unanswered.

Before proceeding to a critical dismantling of these images, in such a way as to be able to demonstrate both their flaws and their permanent validity, it will be helpful to indicate their symbolic, mythical character. To say, for example, that redemption issues from a struggle waged by Christ with the devil, or that redemption consists in paying a ransom to God for an offense committed against God, and so on, are obviously figures of speech, uttered in an attempt to enunciate a transcendent, suprahistorical reality. In times past this language was not always considered mythical and symbolic. It was understood literally, as factual narrative. There was actually a struggle between Christ and Satan, it was thought, or a ransom was really paid. For daughters and sons of modernity and of language science, the myth has been demythologized. But it has not lost its function. It has merely been elevated to the rank of symbol, of a semantic substructure underlying the revelation of realities that can be expressed only symbolically, such as God and redemption, sin and pardon, and so forth. Paul Ricoeur put it very well when he called the symbolic function of myth "its power to disclose the human bond with the Sacred." Unless this bond appears in our analysis, we shall have lost the connection with the past and its language.

FIRST MODEL: EXPIATORY SACRIFICE FOR THE SINS OF HIS PEOPLE

It was not until the writing of the Letter to the Hebrews that our faith tradition interpreted Christ's death as an expiatory sacrifice for our iniquities, and saw confirmation of this interpretation in Isaiah: "He was pierced for our offenses . . . by his stripes we were healed" (53:5). "The Lord laid upon him the guilt of us all" (v. 7). "He was . . . smitten for the sin of his people" (v. 8). "Through his suffering, my servant shall justify many, and their guilt he shall bear" (v. 11).

This model is drawn from the ritual experience of sacrificial worship in a temple. Through their sacrifices, besides worshiping God, human beings thought they were appeasing God's wrath, a wrath provoked by their wickedness. And God became kindly and well-disposed once more. Of course, no human sacrifice sufficed to placate the divine wrath altogether. Then the incarnation created the possibility of a perfect, spotless sacrifice that would win God's entire good pleasure. Jesus freely undertook to be the sacrifice that would represent all men and women before God and win them God's total forgiveness. It was as if the anger of God had reached its paroxysm in Jesus' violent death on the cross and then subsided. Jesus submitted to his death as an expiation and punishment for the sin of the world.

Shortcoming

As long as there was a sociological base for bloody, expiatory sacrifices, as in the Roman or the Judaic culture, this model was perfectly comprehensible. But with the disappearance of this concrete experience, it began to be problematic, and called for a process of dismantling and reinterpretation. Jesus himself, following the prophetic tradition, places the emphasis not on sacrifices and holocausts (Mark 7:7; 12:33; Heb. 10:5–8), but on mercy and goodness, justice and humility. God does not desire what human beings possess. God desires the persons themselves, their heart and their love.

The vindictive, bloody aspect of sacrifice does not accord very well with the image of God revealed to us by Jesus Christ, the image of God as our Father. God is not a wrathful God, but a God who loves the ungrateful and the wicked (Luke 6:35). God is love and forgiveness. God does not wait for sacrifices before offering grace. God takes the initiative, anticipates human beings. And then God surpasses in benevolence everything human beings could ever imagine or wish for.

For Jesus Christ, to open oneself to God meant to abandon oneself to God as a child to a parent. Here is authentic, genuine sacrifice. All persons are sacrifices to the extent that they give this gift of themselves, to the extent that they accept their mortality, sacrificing themselves, spending themselves, dedicating their existence, their time, and their energies to generating a life more liberated, more open to others and to God. All persons are sacrifices, to the extent that they host death in life. Death is not the last atom of life. It is of the very structure of life. Life is mortal. Little by little we die in our very living, until at last our dying and living are done. To host death in life is to accept the corruptibility of existence not as biological fatality, but as an opportunity for the exercise of freedom, in freely giving up this life of mine that is being torn away from me. I must not let life be snatched from me by a biological process. I freely accept life's fixed frontier. I surrender my life, consecrate it, to God and others. The last instant of my mortal life only terminates and formalizes the structure that by now has marked my whole personal history. Now I transport myself to the wealth of the Other, in an expression of love and trust. This is the attitude of genuine Christian sacrifice. As Saint Paul says, "I beg of you through the mercy of God to offer your bodies as a living sacrifice holy and acceptable to God, your spiritual worship" (Rom. 12:1). "Body" is the Hebraic expression for "life," and "spiritual" means according to the new reality of the Spirit, the reality bestowed by Christ.

Permanent Value

The notion of sacrifice has very deep roots in human existence. We still use the word colloquially to express a gift of self that "costs," a gift difficult to give:

Evil, suffering, sin, sloth, habit—many of the economic, social, cultural, and political elements that surround us—generally tend to repress the ebullience of life, though we perceive its infinite potential. Through sacrifice we renew our life, and the life of the world. We bring it up to date, as it were. We maintain its tension. And this sacrifice is an expression of love [Dumas, 169].

Tragically, sacrifice came to be identified with its ritual acts and objects, and they no longer expressed a profound conversion to God. It is this conversion that is the heart of true sacrifice: it is this conversion that is unconditional surrender to God. Conversion is merely exteriorized in ritual gestures or victims offered. Saint Augustine summed it up when he called the visible sacrifice a "sacrament"—that is, the visible sign of an invisible sacrifice (*The City of God,* book 10, chap. 5). Without an interior sacrificial attitude, the external sacrifice remains vacuous and vain.

Human life has an ontological structure of sacrifice. In other words, human life is so structured that it becomes genuinely human only when it opens out to communion, gives of itself, dies to itself to be realized in the other. This gift is the only saving sacrifice. We have a beautiful expression of this in Saint John: "The man who loves his life loses it, while the man who hates his life in this world preserves it to life eternal" (John 12:25). God demands this sacrifice always. God demands it, not because divine justice has been outraged and must be appeased, but because *human beings* need it, inasmuch as they can live and subsist in a human way only if they surrender to the Other, only if they empty themselves in order to be filled with divine grace.

This is the sense in which Christ was the sacrifice par excellence. He was a being-for-others to the last extreme. Not only his death, but his whole life was a sacrifice: it was wholly surrender. If we regard only the gory, bloody aspect of Christ's sacrifice, in order to compare it with the ancient sacrifices, we lose sight of what is special in the sacrifice of Christ. Christ would have been a sacrifice even had he never been immolated, had never shed his blood. This is not what sacrifice is. Sacrifice is self-donation: the total gift of life and death. This gift may assume the character of a violent death, and the shedding of one's blood, historically. But it is not the blood, it is not the violence, that constitute the sacrifice. These only exteriorize the interior sacrifice, which consists of a life project in total availability to God, a life of unconditional surrender to the design of Mystery.

Human life, then, is sacrificially structured. This is what legitimates the assertion that life has manifested itself definitively and eschatologically in Jesus Christ. Jesus Christ is the perfect sacrifice. He *is* salvation, present. Salvation is complete humanization. Complete humanization is the capacity to abstract from oneself altogether, in radical abandon to God, to the point of being one with God. Sacrifice is the supereminent representation of this dimension. Thus it accomplishes our complete hominization and total salvation. Jesus Christ accomplished this himself, and he invites others, with whom he is in ontological solidarity, to do so as well. To the extent that we succeed in doing so, we are saved.

As is evident, the sacrificial model of Christ's redemptive death enjoys an ongoing validity. It is still full of truth today. It need only be purified of its mythic, pagan overtones.

SECOND MODEL: REDEMPTION AS RANSOM— "CRUSHED FOR OUR INIQUITIES"

Another analogy of salvation through Jesus is bound up with the slave culture of another age. A specified price would be paid to "buy back" a person who had been enslaved. This was called a ransom, and the person ransomed was said to have been "redeemed," from the Latin *emere,* "to buy," and *redimere,* "to buy back," to purchase someone's freedom. Christ's death was regarded as the price demanded by God in ransom for all human beings, held in Satan's snare. We were all captives of the demonic, the alienating, and from this captivity we were powerless to deliver ourselves by our own efforts.

In the nomadic culture of the Bible, redemption includes liberation from hunger and thirst. It signifies an exodus from a situation of want to a situation of abundance. The experience of actual captivity in Egypt is also a factor. To be redeemed is to be swept to freedom from a situation of slavery. Redemption is a concept with ties to spatial and local categories. It is a passage from one place to another.

When it abandoned its nomadic ways, Israel transposed the spatial schema of redemption to a temporal one. God will redeem the people by leading it from a provisional time to a definitive time on the horizon of the future. Now redemption is eschatological. Redemption is a pilgrimage through history, an ongoing process of victory over and liberation from the mechanisms of oppression that dog life at every step. Christ is presented as the one who has already reached the goal, who has gained his freedom from all the weight of the alienation of past history. He is the point Omega toward whom all things converge, the redeemer of the world.

Shortcoming

This model of captivity and rescue seeks to underscore the gravity of human perdition. We were not our own property. We were the possession of something that refused to allow us our authentic being. The inadequacy of this model resides in its conceptualization of our redemption, our ransom, as a transaction taking place only between God and Satan. Human beings are mere spectators, not participants. The salvific drama is suprahistorical.

This is not our experience of redemption. Redemption is not extrinsic to life. The fact is that we have to struggle, we have to offer our lives. We do not feel ourselves to be pawns in a game between God and the devil. We experience the exercise of our freedom. We have to live with our decisions. But we experience our liberty as a captive liberty, and our decisions are ambiguous.

Permanent Value

Despite this intrinsic limitation, the image of redemption as ransom, rescue, has an undeniable element of validity. Even in Christianity, men and women do not have the experience of total liberation. Liberation is born in a profound perception of human captivity. We live in an ongoing enslavement by oppressive social and religious systems. Nor are these systems always impersonal: they are enfleshed in civil or religious persons, usually individuals of good will but too ingenuous to perceive that the wickedness all around them is not only outside their precious system but at its heart as well. The evil they seek to combat is fostered and preserved by ideologies calculated to render intrasystemic injustice plausible and rational. The evil around them rests on the support of ideas popularized through every medium of communication.

Christ has delivered us from this captivity. Driven by a new experience of God and a new human praxis, he appeared among us as a human being who was really free, one who was liberated and liberating. By his violent passion and death, he paid the price of the liberty he had claimed in God's name. He never permitted his personal autonomy to be determined by the alienated and alienating socio-religious status quo. Nor was he a "re-actionary"—someone whose behavior is determined purely in response to the world around him or her. The source of Christ's action was a new experience of God and human beings. It was *his* action that provoked re-action, on the part of the official religion that put him to death.

Jesus faced his death honorably, loyally, without compromise or tergiversation, even though he had not sought it, even though it had been forced upon him. His attitude maintains its irresistible "pro-vocative" value even today. It is still capable of rousing the slumbering conscience, of inspiring the enslaved to take up the process of liberation over and over, against all the conformism and cynicism that the regimes of social and religious captivity seem to produce. Christ did not say, "I am the established order and tradition." He said, "I am the truth." And for this truth he was willing to lay down his life, that he might deliver us from the fear of death once and for all. He has vanquished death by his resurrection.

THIRD MODEL: VICARIOUS SATISFACTION— "BY HIS BRUISES WE ARE HEALED"

A juridical mentality borrowed a concept from Roman law to express the redemptive action of Christ: the concept of satisfaction. Introduced by Tertullian and developed by Saint Augustine, this model achieved its classic formulation in Saint Anselm's *Cur Deus Homo?* ("why did God become a human being?"). We note in Anselm a strong tendency—latent, for that matter, in all scholasticism—to rationalism. Anselm's concern is to discover a necessary reason for the incarnation of God that will satisfy even an unbeliever. Theologian Anselm argues as follows. By sin, the human being has violated the right order of creation, and thereby offended God, the author of that universal order. The divine justice demands that this order be healed and restored. Satisfaction will have to be condign. But the offense is infinite: it touches the infinite God. How can a finite human being make infinite reparation? The situation seems hopeless.

Anselm sees a perfectly rational solution. The human being owes God infinite satisfaction. Only God can achieve infinite satisfaction. Therefore God must become a human being. The God-man will be able to render infinite satisfaction. As a human being, God will be able to do what a human being must do: make reparation. As God, a human being will be able to make up for what is lacking in human reparation: infinitude. The God-man will be able to offer infinite (as God) reparation (as a human being). Now the reparation will be condign—equivalent in value to the fault, infinite though that fault be. The logic is faultless. The incarnation is necessary.

And yet what actually repairs the offense is not Christ's incarnation and life. These are only the indispensable prerequisites for a genuine, condign reparation in the form of a bloody death on the cross. By this death the offense is expiated, removed, and the right order of the universe is restored. Indeed, Anselm assures us, God actually regards Christ's death on the cross as beautiful, for it is here that divine justice is appeased (*Cur Deus Homo?*, book 1, chap. 14).

Shortcoming

This representation of Jesus Christ's liberation is one of those most marked by the social substrate of a determinate age. Saint Anselm's God bears little resemblance to the Father of Jesus. He epitomizes the figure of the absolute feudal lord, the master with the power of life and death over his vassals. God is endowed with the traits of a cruel, bloodthirsty judge, bound and determined to exact the last farthing owed by any debtor in justice. A horrible cruelty prevailed in Saint Anselm's time regarding the repayment of debts. This sociological context is reflected in Anselm's theological text, unfortunately contributing to the development of an image of a cruel, sanguinary, vindictive God, an image still present in many tormented, enslaved Christian minds.

A savage mechanism that fits the punishment to the crime is imposed on God, dictating what God must do. Is this the God we learn to love and trust from the experience of Jesus Christ? Is this still the God of the parable of the prodigal son, the God of forgiveness? Is this the God of the lost sheep, who leaves the ninety-nine in the fold and traverses hill and dale in search of the one lost sheep? If God finds death so lovely, then why has he forbidden killing (Exod. 20:13; Gen. 9:6)? How can God, who forbids anger (Matt. 5:21), be angry?

Permanent Value

Saint Anselm is thematizing for theology the only mentality possible in the feudal society of his time. But he fails to uncover the ontological dimension that could have provided an adequate basis for translating into human concepts the salvation achieved by Jesus Christ. This ontological basis appears in response to the question: In what does human salvation basically consist? And the answer, simply put, is: in becoming ever more and more themselves. If they attain this, they will be totally realized, and saved. Here is where the drama of existence begins. Men and women feel incapable of total self-identification. They feel lost. They always owe themselves something. They fail to satisfy the demands they experience within themselves. They feel unsatisfied, incomplete, unfinished. Their situation is unsatisfactory, incapable of completing them.

How must men and women be in order to be completely themselves, and hence saved and redeemed? They must be able to actualize the inexhaustible openness that they themselves are. Their historical trauma consists in their being closed in upon themselves, so that they live in the decaying condition known as sin.

Christ was the individual to whom God granted the measure of openness to the absolute that enabled him to identify with that Absolute. Christ opened himself to each and all. He was without sin—that is to say, he was not convoluted in upon himself. He alone, then, succeeded in satisfying the exigencies of human ontological openness. Thus God could be completely transparent in him (cf. John 14:20). He was the image of the invisible God in bodily form (Col. 1:15; 2 Cor. 4:4).

God did not take flesh in Jesus of Nazareth merely to divinize women and men. God did so to humanize them, as well, and in humanizing them to deliver them from the burden of inhumanity that weighed on them from their historical past. In Jesus there at least emerged the really saved, redeemed human being. Only he, in the power of the Spirit, was able to realize the fullness of human nature. Therefore was he constituted our savior, in the measure of our share in him, in the measure of our actualization of the complete openness that he has made possible, in hope, for all. He has shown that this is not an anthropological utopia, but a historical event of grace.

We can accept Saint Anselm's concern for the necessity of the incarnation of God, and we can make the following proposition. In order for the human being to be really a human being, God had to become incarnate. That is, God had to penetrate the infinite human openness in such a way as to fill it to the full. And now human beings must respond, by expanding their dimensions to those of the Infinite, so that they may fulfill themselves where alone it is possible for them truly to do so: in God. When this occurs, both the incarnation of God and the divinization of the human being occur, and human beings are saved. Now they have answered the deepest call of their being, the call that is the raison d'être of their existence: to be in communion with God, to *be* communion with God.

Christ our savior stirs us, to achieve what he has achieved. We are redeemed, we are satisfied, only to the extent that we are earnest in satisfying our basic human calling. Christ has shown us that our insatiable quest for our ultimate identity—which implies God—is not senseless, as it seemed to be with Sisyphus or Prometheus. There is an end to the quest. Men and women can be what they should be.

It seems to me that, understood in this ontological dimension, the notion of satisfaction can be regarded as a priceless tool for the representation of the liberation offered by Jesus Christ. It is surely because of its inherent wealth that it is one of the most popular images of Jesus Christ's redemption. We experience a solidarity with Jesus in his suffering and in his quest—a solidarity with him who, in the name of all, satisfied the call to complete intimacy with God. And we feel this solidarity in both the earnestness of Jesus' desire and his confidence of our success.

All our images of redemption attempt to capture a salvific wealth beyond the reach of any one image. We must strip them, dismantle them, enlarge them, to take them up once more, purified. Then we must develop any others that may be available to us, against a background of a faith experience incarnate in our own concrete situations.

It remains for me to broach a very ticklish problem mentioned above. How to comprehend the universal character of the liberation wrought by Christ? How is he in solidarity with us, and how does his salvific reality touch our reality, saving and liberating it?

JESUS CHRIST: LIBERATOR IN SOLIDARITY
WITH ALL HUMANKIND

Jesus Christ is not the universal savior by virtue of some pure divine voluntarism, as if this were the way it is simply because this is the way God wants it. There is a deeper reason, one that we verify in our actual experience. We human beings experience a profound sense of solidarity. No one is an island. Now, this unity, this oneness of one and the same humanity, can be adequately explained only against a background of a universal solidarity of origin and destiny. We are together in the solidarity of a life lived in one and the same material cosmos, we are together in solidarity in the same biological process, we are together in solidarity in the same human history of successes and failures, of love and hatred, of violent divisions and a striving for universal fellowship—this history of our relationship with the Transcendent, called God. Thanks to this radical, ontological solidarity, we are all responsible for one another, in salvation and in perdition. "The commandment of love of neighbor was not given to us that we might 'get on better' with our neighbors near and far, or that we might have a more agreeable life. The commandment of love of neighbor is the proclamation of a concern for one another's salvation, and of the possibility of reciprocal salvation."

From the moment we are born into this world, we find ourselves in solidarity with that world. It penetrates us to the quick. We share in its sin and its grace, in the spirit of its times, in the problems and anxieties of all its inhabitants. And conversely: we leave our mark on it. We help to create the world around us.

And we do this not only at the level of human and cultural interrelationships, but also where the position and attitude of persons before God is concerned, helping to determine whether that attitude shall be one of openness and acceptance, or one of closure and rejection.

The manner of existence specific to the human being—spirit—unlike the manner of being of mere things, never permits a human being to remain "on the sidelines," as it were. Persons are always in the midst of personal action, whatever that action be. To be a human being, spirit, is to be capable of becoming, in a way, all things. Our relationship to things, through knowledge and love, founds a communion with and a share in the object known and loved. No one can replace anyone else, it is true. A human being is not an object, an interchangeable something, but a personal, unique, inimitable singularity, historical and free. Nevertheless, in virtue of universal human solidarity, we can place ourselves at one another's service, join our lot to our neighbor's lot, and so have a share in everyone's drama of existence. Thus when we live in a way worthy of a human being, we exalt all other persons, in solidarity with ourselves. When we sink into the abyss of a negation of our humanity, we drag all other persons down to our own level, again in solidarity. We live in solidarity with the wise, the saints, the mystics of all times, by whom salvation and the mystery of God's self-communication have been mediated. But we also live in solidarity with the criminals and malefactors of the ages, by whom the human salvific atmosphere has been contaminated and polluted.

Now, this universal, ontological solidarity also includes Jesus Christ and his liberating action. The theology of the primitive church perceived this very early, as we see in the genealogies of Jesus Christ that subsume the history of Israel (Matt. 1:1–17), the history of the world (Luke 3:23–38), and even the history of the interior life of God (John 1:1–14). Jesus of Nazareth, in the concretion of his personal journey, by the deed and grace of Mystery, accepted God, and was accepted by God, in such a way that God formed a unity with him, without confusion, without separation. This unity was a concrete oneness, not an abstract one, a unity manifested and actualized in the everyday life of the carpenter of Nazareth and the itinerant prophet of Galilee, in his proclamations, in the altercations he provoked, in the deadly conflict he underwent—all the way to the cross—and in resurrection. The historical route traversed by Jesus of Nazareth comprised both God's maximal self-revelation, and the maximal revelation of the openness of a human being. The historical route traversed by Jesus is the pinnacle of human history, and it is irreversible and eschatological—that is, it represents the terminal point of the human process in the direction of God. Here is a oneness between God and the human being without loss of identity on either part. Here is point Omega—our maximal hominization, and the maximal plenitude of our salvation and liberation.

Jesus of Nazareth is in ontological solidarity with our history, and we share, through him and like him, in this point Omega, this situation of salvation and liberation. Therefore faith proclaims him the universal liberator and savior. In him the most radical anthropological structures, the locus of convergence of all our longings for oneness, reconciliation, communion, liberation, and intimacy with the Mystery that permeates our existence, spring into full bloom, achieve their maximal realization. Herein is the secret, profound meaning of the resurrection of Jesus Christ. Christ, achieving the goal, strikes to the root of the being of all human beings, whether they are aware of it or not, indeed even if they reject the proclamation of this good news. Thanks to his solidarity with them in the same humanity, when he touches them he opens to them the possibility of redemption and liberation, he inspires them with a project for the liberation of all their exiled sisters and brothers, he activates the forces that can shake off the yoke of all manner of servitude.

We have already seen how these ideas are verified in the history of the life of Jesus of Nazareth. They were all verified in a liberation story: the story of the life of Jesus Christ. They are meaningful only in an ever-renewed confrontation with the matrix whence they issued. Thus we may hope that they will cease to look and to sound like ideologies, or like harmless words of consolation in the face of frustrated hopes.

Chapter 8

Cross and Death in Theology Today

We have been examining some of the principal historical and systematic problems arising out of the phenomenon of Christ's cross and death. In this chapter I propose to give these considerations a more systematic organization, and locate them within the purview of a current debate raging in theology.

STILL AN OPEN QUESTION . . .

A glance at history reveals the stubborn presence of an antihistory—a history of evil, suffering, violence, and crime of immense dimensions. The problem is not so much that of physical, cosmic evil—the violent, destructive turbulence of the sea, hurricanes, fire, earthquake, birth defects, and so on. The real problem is the prevalence of voluntary evil—the violence wrought by human being upon human being, by one group upon another group. There is a surfeit of aggressiveness in modern societies and human activity. The volume of voluntary evil in the world is so staggering that it becomes a challenge to anthropological meditation.

Pain accompanies growth. Pain can be a relative evil, outweighed by the good achieved through it. But there is another evil, another pain. Evil and pain can be the fruit of human stupidity, or a measureless hatred in the human heart. Some evils, some suffering, are intentionally caused. Indeed evil has a history of its own: the history of the passion of this world, embodied in ideologies, structures, and social dynamisms calculated to generate violence, humiliation, and collective murder.

Some evil, some death, violent though it be, can be regarded positively. There are individuals who suffer from the evil they themselves have wrought in the world. There is a sense of retribution in their suffering, a sense of just punishment due those who have committed evil against others and who now see that evil turned back upon themselves.

But there is also the evil, and the death, inflicted on persons who have had only love for the world, individuals who have devoted their lives to the fashioning of a more human, more humane world. They have "proclaimed and

102

denounced," have heralded good and decried evil wherever they saw the need to do so. They have carried forward their grand project of reconciliation, dreaming a world where it would be easier to be brothers and sisters to one another, a world in which love would be less difficult. These persons, too, have suffered violent deaths. These are the victims of closed societies, and they are struck down by ideologies devoted to the protection of the privileges of selfish groups. They died in their innocence, the victims of the very hatred they sought to overcome. As the author of the Letter to the Hebrews says, with profound sorrow, and yet with profound hope:

> Still others endured mockery, scourging, even chains and imprisonment.
> They were stoned, sawed in two, put to death at sword's point; they went
> about garbed in the skins of sheep or goats, needy, afflicted, tormented.
> The world was not worthy of them. They wandered about in deserts and
> on mountains, they dwelt in caves and in holes of the earth. Yet despite
> the fact that all of these were approved because of their faith, they did not
> obtain what had been promised [Heb. 11:36–39].

They did not obtain the promised better world. They died. They were killed. Their deaths appear absurd and meaningless. What meaning can there possibly be in "the blood of all the prophets shed since the foundation of the world" (Luke 11:50)? What meaning can there be in the murder of numberless, nameless peasants and workers, struggling for a life of humanity and dignity for themselves and others, and cut down by the swords of the proud and mighty? Who will raise them up? The Lord tells us, "This generation will have to account for the blood of all the prophets" (Luke 11:50). Yes, but when? Is there any possible hope for this tortured human existence of ours?

This is the context of the passion and cross of Jesus Christ. The problems are:

1. The murderer
2. The crucified victim
3. The vicarious, sacrificial victim
4. God who permits this crime and this suffering
5. God who takes up his cross, suffers, and dies

Christian faith presents Jesus Christ in death, nailed to the cross and raised again, as the one who has taken upon himself all the great problems arising out of the thematic of evil, such as sin, such as the cross as the mystery of the passion of human history. Jesus Christ suffered the violence of his age. He bore his cross and died on it freely. He bore it as a sacrifice for others. All this fell in with God's plan, which respects human beings' freedom and history. And finally, the one who died was the very Son of God, so that we may say: God died on the cross.

This process, lived and undergone in its entirety by the Son of Man and the Son of God, delivered the world from the absurdity of the cross, delivered the world from death. It transformed death and the cross into an opportunity for redemption and encounter with God. This is what we profess, in Christian faith.

Before I subject each of the five points of this problematic to a brief examination, let us consider certain modern approaches to the ensemble.

THEOLOGIES OF THE CROSS TODAY

The cross has always been part and parcel of Christian faith, piety, and theology. Without it the good news of the resurrection would hold no hope, for it would hold no content. The one who was raised up is precisely the one who had been crucified. However, not all the implications of the cross and death of Christ have always been given the emphasis they merit. A modern, radical approach to the faith in light of the cross has been undertaken by theologians Jürgen Moltmann, a Protestant, and Hans Urs von Balthasar, a Catholic. But they are not the only ones to have done so. The modern experience of the pain of the world has called forth other understandings of the cross, as well, all in an attempt to allow the light of the passion of Christ to fall on that pain and bestow meaning on the meaningless.

Jesus Christ, the Crucified God

Moltmann begins with a thesis profoundly rooted in the Lutheran tradition. An authentic Christian theology, he says, must be practiced in the shadow of the cross. Christians find their identity in the cross. No one can love pain and suffering. Yet the Christian follows and proclaims a crucified Lord. Because it failed to keep the cross at the center of Christianity, the church sought its identity in rites, dogmas, and traditions.

Even on the level of practice there is an identity problem. The specifying characteristic of Christians is not that they strive for a better world. This they do, yes, but so do many others today, driven by a wide variety of ideologies and inspirations. But there is a difference. Even were we one day to succeed in setting up a classless society—the project of practically all the modern libertarian movements—Christians will still be identified by the cross, which makes them insane as far as the wise are concerned, a scandal to "religious" persons, and a thorn in the side of the powerful. Both the verticalism of prayer and the horizontalism of love, which converge in the transformation of the world, collapse before the cross. Everything, Moltmann goes on, is called into question: a God who is deaf to Jesus' mighty prayer, a God who is seen to be incapable of seconding Jesus' great commitment as he passed through the world doing good and transforming human relationships. The theology of the cross crucifies the Christian. It questions all our models, our representations of the human being, God, and society. It obliges the Christian to embrace an identity that cannot be projected as a political or religious model of an immanent future in history. It destroys all this—and leaves men and women as naked as Christ on the cross.

This is Moltmann's vision of the reality of the cross, and it is within this vision that he seeks to situate Jesus' death. What is the essence of the cross, and therefore of the Christian? Moltmann contemplates Jesus' trial, in which he is sentenced as a blasphemer and messianic seducer, and observes: Jesus' death is the consequence of a life led in strict accord with his principles. And yet it is not enough to say that Christ died as a prophet or a martyr. This much is true, of course. But it falls short of the ultimate, crucial truth that identifies Christ and thereby the Christian as well. What truth? We find it in Jesus' rejection by God. Besides being rejected by the civil and religious authorities, the Son of God is rejected by his own Father. Jesus' cry of abandonment and despair on the cross translates this rejection. Jesus suffered the absolute absence of God, and sank into the torments of hell. Jesus' death meant the end of his cause, the failure of his proclamation. Here is what is specific to Jesus' cross. Here is what distinguishes that cross from all the other crosses of history.

This conceptualization, Moltmann goes on, destroys all our previous notions of God. No longer is God the fullness of Being, who defends us against all who seek to destroy us. Now God is a God who annihilates. All this is clear in a whole series of paradoxes: God's grace in sinners, God's justice in the evil, God's divinity in one crucified. God is revealed not in power, but in impotence. Thus the God of Jesus Christ is the God who destroys all human images of God. They are all idolatrous. Moltmann, therefore, in the spirit of Barth, finds fault with all types of traditional religion, Christian or non-Christian. They all fail the test of the cross, the crucible in which they are ground to powder.

Who dies on the cross? The victim is Jesus the Son of God. And so the cross, and death, are bonded to the being of God. Death impinges on God. Hence the title of Moltmann's book, *The Crucified God*. God is subject and object alike. God crucifies and is crucified. God crucifies the Son, cursing him and rejecting him. And the Son dies an abandoned God. God suffers the death of the Son, in the pain of love. In Jesus, then, God too is crucified and dies. The death of Christ, the Son of God, actualizes God's capacity for death, for being crucified. On the cross, then, we have the Holy Trinity: the rejecting Father, the abandoned Son, and the Spirit as the power by which all this takes place and is maintained in unity.

Thus God assumes the passion of the world. Human suffering is no longer exterior to God. It transpires within God. Still, Moltmann cautions, we must not think that death, and the reasons for death, such as hatred and violence, are eternalized, merely because now they are God's. Instead, God must be thought of as being in process. God is vulnerable. God can change. After all, God can suffer and God can love. In the end, when God will achieve full identity, and the Son will surrender his reign to the Father, then God will be all in all, and evil and death will no longer prevail. God will have overcome rejection, murder—crucifying and being crucified. God will be in glory.

God's No to Suffering

In his work, *Wider die Versöhnung Gottes mit dem Elend: eine Kritik des christlichen Theismus und A-theismus* ("against God's reconciliation with misery: a critique of Christian theism and a-theism"), Ulrich Hedinger sketches a line of thought altogether different from Moltmann's. Hedinger's basic thesis is that suffering is not to be accepted, it is to be combated. Any attempt to justify suffering that would implicate God as causing or permitting it, far from pointing a way toward a solution, merely aggravates the problem. The theistic solution, in the concept of God as an almighty Father, is forced to keep suffering at an infinite distance from God. The dialectical solution, positing the alternation-in-simultaneity of death and life, neutralizes death theoretically, but fails to account for the evil of crime, of hate. This evil is not subsumed in a higher synthesis. A nonidentity, a total absurdity, is verified within the dialectical process. Finally, the Christian a-theism of so many theologians who maintain that Jesus was crucified in God's stead, that God might suffer with human beings vicariously, likewise fails as a theodicy, eternalizing evil instead of eliminating it.

There can be legitimation of evil, Hedinger maintains. God's reign is one of felicity, not of the integration of evil. The spirituality of the cross is "dolorism"—a vain effort of mortification in order to conjure away the evil of the world. No, the world will be free, the world will be good, only in the eschaton. Until then, the world is in a process of *creatio in fieri* ("creation in the course of becoming"), and evil endures. Evil is the "not yet" of the reign of God. Sin is the refusal to grow, to develop, to overcome our imperfections, to cooperate with God that creation may not be the creation of God alone but of human effort as well.

Rather than attribute evil to God, Hedinger opts for a dualism. All sublimation of suffering and evil—Moltmann's solution—is sheer cruelty. Suffering cannot be the focal datum of the history of love. Such a notion is verifiable neither in human experience nor in the experience we have of God. On the contrary, God is love. God is not self-cancer, God is not in revolt against God. *Deus contra Deum!* ("God against God"), cries Hedinger in exasperation (Moltmann's solution). The destruction of another is never experienced as a manifestation of love. Christ's death is a crime of political murder. Jesus did not have to die on the cross in order to manifest the love of God his Father. His death is the fruit of a life of fidelity to his Father.

We may not say, then, concludes Hedinger, that God is the author of evil and good, of dereliction and of love. The Father's rejection of his Son would mean a loveless God. However, we may say that God suffers with us, and suffers in Jesus Christ, that God is in solidarity with Jesus' suffering and ours, that God is suffering too, to deliver us from suffering, introducing the universe to a kind of love that willingly assumes suffering and death, not because it perceives some value in it, but in order to render it impossible from within. Just as creation is still en route to its identity, and so not all evil has been overcome, so also God is en route to identity. When creation has burst into God, then God too will have achieved full realization and fulfillment.

Our Task: A Meaning for Meaningless Suffering

The book by the fine Protestant lay theologian Dorothee Sölle, *Suffering,* is a frank polemic, directed particularly against Moltmann. For Sölle, suffering has no meaning; but we can endow it with meaning. There is a suffering that we can conquer. There is also a suffering before which we are powerless. In the face of profound suffering, all words are empty, all expression is betrayal. There is nothing for it but to fall silent in the presence of an apophatic mystery. Suppose God were to intervene and stay the martyrdom of an innocent child. Would this be an answer for us? Surely not. We can address only the suffering that we can change, or from which we can learn. The suffering and death that we take upon ourselves in line with our task to diminish the suffering of the world is suffering and death with meaning. The Christian is not a stoic, passively observing while the evils of the world prosper. Christians react positively, Christians rebel against evil, bending all their efforts to overcome it.

What is the relationship of suffering to God? Sölle wisely observes that God does not send suffering as a punishment or as a test of obedience. Only an arbitrary, anthropomorphic God would do that. God does not torture. God does not will suffering. God is not a sadist. God favors our struggle against suffering. The suffering born of that struggle is a suffering endowed with human dignity, and endorsed by God.

Sölle concludes with a severe criticism of Moltmann, as we shall see below. She also refuses to attempt to reconcile God with misery. "He who does not weep needs no utopia; to him who only weeps God remains mute" (Sölle, 166). Men and woman must take up the challenge of suffering, in order to generate love and accept love, even at the cost of pain.

Memoria Passionis

The theology of Johannes B. Metz has been a theology in flux. From an anthropologico-existential theology (*Christian Anthropocentrism,* 1962), Metz moved first to a theology of secularization (*Theology of the World,* 1966), then to a political theology (from 1967).

Beginning in 1969, Metz thematizes the *memoria passionis* ("memory of suffering"), insisting that it calls for a new method of doing theology. Metz calls for a "narrative theology" to counterbalance a "theology of argumenta-tion" (from 1972). The content of Christian theology, he explains, cannot be articulated exclusively against a concordistic, argumentative background; nor again can a dialectical method supply the equations for problems and contra-dictions of a historical and social nature. There is always an antithetical element not subsumed in the transcendent synthesis: there is an evil that is "no good at all." There is such a thing as pure wickedness, unmitigated malice.

The history of the victims of murder and injustice cannot be mended. They stand in history as a permanent denunciation of *homo emancipator*—anyone who pretends to make linear historical progress without sacrifices. This is where the *memoria passionis* enters the scene—the dangerous, subversive memory of the humiliated and the wronged, of those who were vanquished but whose memory can stir up "dangerous" visions, and launch new liberation movements.

For Metz, this is the story of Jesus. There is no argumentation. Simply, a story is told. This story, this history, shatters all the totalities that seek to incorporate evil, suffering, sin, as a function of a higher mechanism. There is a negativity that does not admit of reconciliation. There is a negativity with no present meaning whatever. But this negativity can have a future. And it is this future that is revealed in the risen Jesus Christ. Crucified, murdered, Jesus Christ rises again. And thus he solves the enigma of history: the slaughtered, from the beginning of time until now, live—as does Jesus.

Thus the *memoria passionis* becomes a *memoria resurrectionis*. Meaning is not the monopoly of conquerors. The resurrection reveals another kind of meaning—the future of those whose lot it has been to be the *massa damnata,* those forgotten by history, the excluded. The church, then, which bonds these two memories into one, is not an argumentative community, but a narrative one—the reviver of memories. The church is living memory. The church is the gospel alive in the life of the church. But the church must do its recounting and narrating also, its recalling and remembering, in such a way as to function as the unmasker of totalitarian ideologies. The church is not dispensed from argumentation, as an apologetic to defend the narrative and apply it to each new situation.

The Cross: Not a Problem to Be Solved, but a Scandal to Be Shouldered

Hans Urs von Balthasar refuses to have recourse to reason to transcend the scandal of the cross for all human thought. The cross *is* scandal. The cross is cross precisely to the extent that it continues to be scandal. In an intellectual framework it ceases to be cross. It becomes a function of another reality instead, and so is undone in its own reality as scandalous cross.

The incarnation, says von Balthasar, is per se of the order of passion. Christ's incarnation is oriented to his passion. Incarnation means that God assumes the totality of human experience. But human experience includes the experience of sin and hell. Christ assumed all this, then, all through his life, to his very death—all the way to the experience we all have of abandonment by God, all the way to a descent into hell, or the experience of absolute condemnation. Thus the passion of this world is transformed into the passion of Jesus Christ. This *kenosis* forces us to correct our image of God, which has been distorted by the static Greek conception of a *Deus immobilis.*

Tradition makes two basic assertions. First, the supreme *kenosis* of the cross is glory (Saint John: death is twofold elevation, elevation on a cross and elevation to glory). Second, through the incarnation God not only redeemed the world, but revealed the furthest depths of the divine nature. The incarnation has affected God, then, for God has imparted new self-revelation. God has revealed, in effect, that world and incarnation must be "thought intratrinitarily." It is no longer enough to conceive of world and incarnation as God's work *ad extra*. On this premise, the conclusion is ineluctable: in taking on human flesh and the human condition, God, the divine Trinity, takes on suffering and death. And when God dies on the cross—because God remains God—death becomes a form of God. God's omnipotence consists in being able to do everything, not in being able to avoid everything. God's immutability consists in being able to change completely. In other words, the changeless element in God is God's constant change and process.

There is a theological truth that stands midway between an immutability of God so static that the incarnation is altogether external to divinity, and a mutability of God such that Jesus' self-consciousness is totally alienated from God's, and altogether relegated to the realm of human consciousness. And this theological truth is: the lamb immolated from the beginning of the world (cf. Rev. 13:8; 5:6; 9, 12). Concretely: Jesus Christ's earthly pilgrimage must be situated within the eternal plan of God, which is an all-comprehensive plan, embracing suffering, death, and the cross. All of this belongs to the eternal Son. He takes all of this upon himself when he becomes incarnate.

Our image of God must change, then. We must broaden our horizons of understanding when we speak of the world and history. We must no longer understand these as exterior to God. We must look upon the world and its history as existing and transpiring within God's trinitarian process. Then we shall see that God can change. Changes in the world are only the worldly form of the changes of God.

God must be sought *sub contrario*. Where God seems not to be, where God seems to have withdrawn, there we shall find God most intensively present. This logic contradicts the logic of reason. This is the logic of the cross. The logic of the cross is a scandal to reason, and must be maintained as such. Only thus shall we have this access to God. Otherwise we should never surmise it. Reason seeks the cause of suffering. Reason seeks reasons for evil. The cross seeks no causes. God is to be found in suffering, and most intensively of all. Where reason sees the absence of God, the logic of the cross sees God's full revelation.

Then von Balthasar moves on to a fierce attack on any philosophy that would seek to make of the cross a principle of universal intellection. The cross is nothing of the kind, says von Balthasar. The cross must remain the cross: the blind spot in the eye of the reasoning and the wisdom of the world.

The hiatus between the cross and the wisdom of this world is bridged only in the resurrection as eschatological reality. Here is where we see the life of the cross revealed in its full light. The resurrection is the deed not of the light of reason, but of the darkness of death. This is why it is the crucified one who rises, and not Apollo, not Jupiter, not someone in glory who passes to an even greater glory. The one who rises is the one who was abandoned, the one who was rejected. Why? Because within abandonment and rejection is a different sort of life, a life fully divine: resurrection. Indeed, according to von Balthasar, it is resurrection that represents the unity of the trinitarian process itself.

In light of the trinitarian process, the cross is more than the Son's cross alone. Now the cross touches all three divine persons: the Father, as principal agent; the Son, as the one who, in solidarity with human beings, experiences what it means to say no to God, without God's having said no (Heb. 4:15); and the Holy Spirit as the reconciliation of all, of the Father with the Son and of creation with God.

The Cross: Scandalous Because Criminal

The reflections of the theology of liberation on the historical and salvific meaning of the cross focus mainly on the dimension of salvation as incarnation:

> Our theology of the cross must be historical. Rather than viewing the cross as some arbitrary design on God's part, we must see it as the outcome of God's primordial option: the incarnation. The cross is the outcome of an incarnation situated in a world of sin that is revealed to be a power working against the God of Jesus [Sobrino, 201-2].

The cross is to be understood as God's solidarity with men and women in the condition of human suffering—not to eternalize it, but to suppress it. And the manner in which God seeks to suppress it is not by domination, but by love. Christ preached and lived this new dimension. He was rejected by a "world" oriented toward the preservation of power. He succumbed to these forces. But he never abandoned his project of love. The cross is the symbol of human power—and the symbol of Jesus' love and fidelity. Love is stronger than death, and power collapses before it. The loyalty of the cross, then, the love on the cross, has triumphed. The name for this is resurrection: a life stronger than the life of power, biological life, the life of the ego.

Can the cross be projected within God? If we mean the cross of love, then yes. But the cross of love is a consequence of the cross of hate. The cross in itself is not a symbol of love or encounter. It is a form of torture. It is the means by which human beings vent the power of their vengeance. This cross, the cross of hate, cannot be projected within God—unless we wish to destroy all possible understanding of God. The God who dies and who rejects the Son is comprehensible only within a theology of love. The rejected one replaces and represents the sinners of the world. He is not rejected because he is the Son. He is rejected because he becomes the sin of the world (2 Cor. 5:21) without having committed sin himself.

The task of faith, and of Christianity organized as a historical force, is to render the hatred that generates the cross ever more impossible, not through violence, which simply forces whatever it wishes, but through love and reconciliation, which vanquishes all humankind.

CONVERGENCES AND DIVERGENCES
IN THE VARIOUS POSITIONS

A God Who Does Not Suffer Does Not Deliver from Suffering

These theological visions are all visions indeed. Perhaps the most theological way to discourse upon radical human problems such as suffering, death, love, life, and so on, is in the language of symbol and myth. These do not explain a great deal. But they "make us think." The solution they indicate is not a formula, not the conclusion of an argument, but a journey we make together, in solidarity, weeping together and consoling one another. This requires us to move away from the notion of a static, a-pathetic (nonsuffering) God to that of a living God, a "pathetic" God (one with pathos, one who can suffer). And all these authors do this. As Bonhoeffer says, a God who does not suffer cannot free us.

But how shall we understand God's suffering? How can we speak about God's suffering?

What Sort of God Can Die?

How must we approach the death of God? Can suffering be predicated of God in such a way as to make God the subject, the cause of pain and suffering, and not merely its object? May we speak of a God who is the agent in the process of suffering? May we say that God causes pain in the world, and not merely that God suffers in solidarity with the pain of the world, suffers the pain of the world because the world suffers? This is the great problem of the cross.

A God who in an unqualified manner is both object and subject of death, a God who dies and who causes death, will be the God of a deeply ambiguous, primitive theological discourse. Moltmann's language betrays a *profound* lack of theological rigor. Moltmann's God is epiphanic. God appears as Pain and Death. Moltmann presents us with a phenomenon of our everyday experience, upon which we may discourse in everyday language. He permits himself an unceremonious discourse about a "revolt of God against God," or of a "disunion in God," or "enmity between God and God," a "God who rejects God, who is against God," or "God abandoned by God," the abandonment of Jesus on the cross as a "positive, excluding act by a Father who grows angry with his Son and rejects him," and so on. We slip into a primitive, mythical form of discourse in the pejorative sense of the term—in the sense of articulation within an objectifying consciousness. We no longer have a theo-logical discourse, our propositions are no longer uttered in an awareness of the ambiguity and ana-logical nature of our discourse upon God. All the most celebrated theologians of the moment are guilty of this naive error.

A God Who Crucifies His Son?

Moltmann's most problematic thesis, and to a great extent that of von Balthasar, is the proposition that the Father effectuated the sacrifice of his Son on the cross. The Father does what Abraham did not do. Abraham did not sacrifice his son Isaac. The Father goes further: he kills his Son. Moltmann is fascinated with such a deed. What a radical theology of the cross! It is no longer the son who kills the father, as in Freudian theory, but the father who kills his son.

Von Balthasar and Moltmann both speak in this way to bring out the scandal of the cross. But it is no longer clear whether the cross is a scandal to human understanding (the religious notions of the Jews or the philosophical ones of the Greeks) or is a scandal so absolute that it must be one for God as well. The entire discourse seems calculated to make a clean break with all possibility of a functional *logos*. All is beyond the reach of verification, by any means whatsoever. We have only raw fact, and hence the most radical dogmatism.

Ultimately this kind of dogmatism is atheistic. Fideism and atheism are cut from the same cloth. If we admit the thesis under consideration, nothing else will be left in the way of either a complete atheism, or a reduction of Christianity to the kind of fanatic dogmatism that asserts itself as sheer will to power. To present this conception of the cross as liberation, and to elevate it to the status of a tribunal critical of any liberation project, is a sure way to universalize slavery. To achieve liberation by making us all slaves of a tyrannical, absurd concept of God devoid of any participation in rationality or light, a concept shrouded in palpable darkness, in pure ignorance and arbitrariness—God, by an eternal decree, has resolved to justify the cross with the cross—is to sacrifice the Lamb to the sheerest determinism.

If propositions like this are defensible in order to explain the scandalous character of the cross, then why may we not move on to still more scandalous assertions, equally devoid of good sense and moderation? Of course we may say: The one who dies is God's Son; therefore death touches God; therefore God dies. Yes, but not *in recto.* God dies only *in obliquo.* Death is a creaturely modality. God did not annihilate the human being when God assumed human nature. God assumed human nature *inconfuse.* God respects the human mode of being. However, in virtue of the intimate union between humanity and divinity in the incarnation, we may say *in obliquo* that God dies. But we must exercise utmost caution here. Jesus smiled, Jesus took nourishment, Jesus digested what he ingested, Jesus experienced the human biological needs of hunger, thirst, the need for sleep, and the need to relieve himself. In Moltmann's logic, we can transform these physiological needs into trinitarian problems! What does it mean, we should have to ask, for God to have biological needs? How is this inserted into the trinitarian process? And we end up transforming trinitarian and christological faith into a chapter pasted together from an ancient mythology and modern pornography. Language has lost its rigor, and degenerated into a purely deductive mechanism of a blind, material interpretation of formulas.

My own position is that when faith, in the reverence of mystical silence, has said, "Jesus is God," it has said all there is to say. After that, silence alone is adequate. Anything else that will be said will be vacuous, superfluous, or redundant. We cannot go on with constructs upon the reality enunciated. We have said all we can. It is the part of theology and of faith simply to demonstrate that the proposition that Jesus is God is not self-contradictory. Neither theology nor faith can then seize upon God as a fixed, stable, rational datum and make deductions from this datum. God would no longer be the God enunciated in the formula, "Jesus is God." God would be an idol, something you can make deductions from.

Once it has performed its apologetical task of demonstrating the noncontradiction of its basic christological formula, the business of theology is to proceed not to a theological systematics of God and human being in combination, but to an ethic of the discipleship of this Jesus who is also God. How may we follow him so as to come ever nearer to him? The route of Western theology has taken a more and more systematic direction, with all the attendant insoluble, false contradictions that are still being debated today. It has failed to elaborate an ethic, a "policy," and so has degenerated into a doctrinaire abstraction, surrendering the duty of an ethical project of the organization of life to the pagan principles of the Nicomachean ethics or the imperatives of state or church as be-all and end-all.

In Moltmann's vision the passion is reduced to a single basic causality: that of God the Father. The causality of Jesus' adversaries, who produced the historical death of Jesus Christ with their moral introversion and self-centeredness, goes by the board. All is subsumed in God. Is it true that God is the cause of Jesus' suffering? This is a question that Sölle asks, for example. No. Jesus suffered freely, for love of the world, society, and all those who suffer, and he died of a longing for the Absolute. The humanization of the suffering of the world is not the fruit of the *fact that* the Son, too, must suffer, but of *how* the Son suffered. If he takes on suffering *for the sake of suffering,* because Suffering is God—because God, too, suffers: God *is* Suffering—then there is no way to overcome suffering. Suffering is eternal. We are lost irrevocably, captives of the dehumanizing dynamisms of Suffering. In this vision the experience of suffering leaves us no hope.

There is a surprising parallelism between this theology, which unloads all the burden of violence on God, and the baleful vision of Nazism. Sölle cites Himmler's address to his SS troops on the occasion of his visit to the Nazi extermination camp at Poznan, Poland:

The majority of you know what it means to fling a hundred, five hundred, a thousand corpses together in a single heap. You have seized the scalpel manfully, you have excised this mass of human degeneration without succumbing to nausea. You are hard, you are strong. This is a glorious page in our history. No one has ever written the like. No one ever will.

The mistake of this theology, which projects suffering and the cross in unqualified fashion onto the very being of God, consists in accepting the proposition that the Father is Jesus' murderer. The divine wrath is unslaked by a vengeance wreaked on God's other daughters and sons, Jesus' sisters and brothers. It must have the firstborn Son. Filicide is promoted to the rank of the sacred theological.

A vision of such macabre dimensions must be refused all Christian legitimacy. It destroys all the newness of the gospel, forcing that gospel into service as an instrument for the sacramentalization of the wickedness of the world. It is not for this that we have been baptized; it is not for this that we have died and risen in Jesus Christ.

The real reason God is silent in the face of suffering is that God is suffering. God takes up the cause of the martyred, of the suffering (cf. Matt. 25:31). God is acquainted with suffering. But God has not undertaken to eternalize it and deprive us of all hope. On the contrary, God has assumed it because God means to put an end to all the crosses of history.

Christianity began as a religion of slaves, proletarians, and the marginalized. It did not begin as a way of eternalizing their situation. Their hope was that Christianity would do away with it. Christian morality is a subversive morality: it seeks to subvert the ruler-slave relationship.

Of what use is suffering? To change and to transform the world? Then it has meaning. It is a divine sorrow (2 Cor. 7:8–10). Is it for annihilation, to reinforce evil? Then it is worldly sorrow, and of no use except for digging your own hell as a punishment for the evil you commit.

The problem of evil is a problem not of theodicy but of ethics. Evil—its burden and its defeat—is understood not by speculating about it, but by taking up a practice of combat for good, by embracing those causes that produce love and deliverance from the crosses of this world.

A Suffering God: How Does God Suffer?

To say that God is love is to say that God is vulnerable. In other words, God loves, and we can accept or reject this God who loves. To say that God is love is to postulate a pole of love from which a dialogue of love with God can be launched. Love occurs only in freedom, and in the encounter of two freedoms. Salvation history shows the human capacity for rejecting love. God is not indifferent to this rejection. God suffers from it. Love, however, does not desire suffering. Love desires felicity. And because it is so supremely desirous of the felicity of the other, it continues to love that other even in the face of that other's rejection. Now love takes up the other's pain, because it loves that other and wishes to share that other's pain. This is the manner of God's suffering: to suffer as the fruit of love and of the infinite capacity of love for solidarity. Moltmann says, and here I agree with him:

> The Trinity is completely in itself and complete in itself. Still, it is open to the world and to human beings, and is "imperfect" in its being of love

inasmuch as the lover does not wish to be perfect without the participation of the beloved [*Theologische Quartalschrift,* 153 (1973) 350].

We must not, however, project upon God the mechanisms that generate suffering, cross, division, and hatred among human beings. In a word, we may not force God and the cross into a bond that would be intrinsic to the divine identity. If we could, we should be lost. If suffering is an expression of God's very essence, if God hates, if God crucifies, then there is no salvation for us. God would be simultaneously good and evil, and we would be the hapless flotsam of the eternal alternation of that good and that evil. How would we speak of a redemption that comes from God, *were God also in need of redemption?*

And yet the cross does affect God. It means the violation of God's historical project of love. It violates God's sacred rights. It means rebellion, it means the establishment of the reign of men and women without God. If God is beyond the cross as hatred, if God has no place in the role of the cross as crime, then God can transform the cross into love. God can make the cross a benediction.

If God were cross, then Jesus' redemption, Jesus' solidarity with the crucified of the world, would be meaningless. In order to suffer, God must assume the other-than-God. The other-than-God, the utterly other with respect to God, is non-God, God's negation, the situation of the cross as crime. If there were cross in God, the incarnation of God would of itself establish the cross, and there would be nothing left for God to "take on." God would merely be revealed for what God already is: cross and suffering. Cross and suffering would be God now projected upon the world. But because God is not cross, God can take up the cross, as something new, even for God. And this is an enormous addition to oneself—even for God. God assumes the cross in order to be-in-solidarity with those who suffer—not to sublimate and eternalize the cross, but to enter into solidarity with those who suffer on the cross and thus transform the cross into a sign of blessing, a sign of suffering love. Love, then, is the motive for this assumption of the cross by God.

Here is the meaning of a God on the cross, a God in pain. Here is the meaning of the teachings of a"pathetic theology." In this vision, courageous poverty, decision, outrage, and suffering win a divine dimension—not to numb our awareness in the struggle with the passion of the world, but to say that only in solidarity with the crucified can we struggle against the cross, only in identification with the victims of tribulation can there be real liberation from tribulation. And this was Jesus' road, the path of God incarnate.

THE CROSS AS THE DEATH OF ALL SYSTEMS

The cross cannot be posited as the generating principle of a system of intellection, as Moltmann and von Balthasar attempt to do. The cross is the death of all systems. It will not fit into a framework. It bursts all bonds. It is the symbol of a total negation. It is sin and rejection of God. It must, therefore, issue from a freedom. The systems I have examined make very little or no mention of human freedom—the enormous freedom to reject God and create hell. The cross springs from a rejection of the reign of God. It is sin, and sin is completely absurd. The cross has no intelligibility, and therefore can never function as a link in a logical, cohesive system. It shatters all, because it breaks with God, who is absolute *Logos*.

And yet, absurd as the cross is, it is still more absurd for God to have taken it up. Here is the decisive factor for our investigation. All truth hangs in the balance here. Absurd as it was for God to assume the cross, this constituted no obstacle for God. God is so great, so utterly beyond any possible negation, that God can undertake to assume the absurd—not to divinize it, not to eternalize it, but to reveal the dimensions of divine glory, which transcend all light coming from the human *logos* and all darkness arising from the human heart.

God assumes the cross in solidarity with and love for the crucified of history, with those who suffer the cross. God tells them, "absurd as it is, the cross can be the pathway of a marvelous liberation. But you must take it up in freedom and love. Then you will deliver the cross from its absurdity, and yourself from yourself. You are greater, and you become greater, than the cross. For liberty and love are greater than all absurdities, and stronger than death. For you can make them, too, your road to me."

And so the cross enters the history of love, the history of what love can do with its potential for solidarity. The cross is the locus of revelation of the sublimest form of love. Here love betrays its essence. The essence of love is realized in the power to be in the other as other, the utterly other. The utterly other than myself is my enemy. To love my enemy—the cross—to be on that cross, to take up that cross, is the deed of love. Here is the essence of love. The cross, once it is taken up in freedom and love, realizes the human being totally, imparting the opportunity to love in the most sublime manner. The cross itself is neither love nor the fruit of love. It is the place where the power of love is shown. The cross is hatred destroyed by a love that takes up the cross and the hatred. This is liberation.

The cross of hatred is mystery, however. It is inaccessible to discursive reason, though capable of realization in human praxis. There is no logical argument to justify a human being's rejection of another human being and of God. And yet it happens. The cross, then, cannot be systematized in a cohesive conception of the world and God. It tears every system to shreds. Thus it is the symbol of our finitude, of the frontiers of our reason. The cross crucifies reason. The cross crucifies theology as a systematic intellection of God and the things of God. The challenge to love this frailty, to understand it as a way of showing another approach to God, through the asssumption of the cross in love, is the great challenge and opportunity offered by the cross to our freedom.

The cross is not there to be understood. It is there to be taken up—to be carried in the footsteps of the Son of Man, who took up his cross and by that cross accomplished our redemption.

Chapter 9

Suffering Born of the Struggle against Suffering

We gain access to the great problems of life and death, suffering and love, not through concepts but through myth, not through argumentation but through narrative. The Western history of reflection on suffering, from the Job of the Bible to the Job of Carl Jung, is the story of the failure of all theoretical solutions, the history of frustration of all concepts. Evil is not there to be understood, but to be combated.

Clearly, the same conclusion is to be drawn from the life story of those who have helped to confer a meaning on suffering, not for the purpose of "getting a handle on it," but for the sake of a struggle against it. They have suffered in the battle against suffering. But their suffering was worthy, rewarding, and profoundly liberative.

MYSTERIUM ET PASSIO LIBERATIONIS

Here is a *passio vitae* of long years ago. Father Carlos Alberto was a country pastor. His parish was in a region where a few large plantations were in the hands of a few exceedingly wealthy families, whereas thousands of semiliterate peasants lived what Dom Hélder Câmara calls the life of Severino:

Severino of the Northeast, son of Severino, grandson of Severino, lives, like those other Severinos, a living death. He does not live; he vegetates. Not like a shady tree with its roots filled with the sap of life, but like his brother the cactus. So far he has not rebelled. From his illiterate parents and in the chapel belonging to his lord and master he has learned to be patient, like the Son of God who was condemned unjustly and died on the cross to save us. In his own way he concludes that things cannot be otherwise. A pupil in the school of Christianity and fatalism, he simply accepts the fact that some are born rich and others poor, and that such is the will of God [Câmara, 22].

117

Father Carlos Alberto came to the realization that the evangelization of his parish would have to include a proclamation of basic human rights, and an effort to defend those rights. Shepherding his parishioners would involve the promotion of their socio-political liberation. How might Father Carlos Alberto show these "nonpersons" the credibility of the Christian message that God was their Father? What structural changes would be needed in their surroundings in order to veri-fy—make true, give meaning to—the message that we are all sisters and brothers?

With great difficulty he began to gather the people in groups. Little grassroots groups gradually took shape. These tiny communities simply read and meditated on passages from the New Testament. There was no ideological indoctrination. Simply, the gospel was brought into their lives. The gospel was applied to life. This made them start thinking. It allowed them to speak their word of truth. It made them aware that they were persons—not things, not animals.

There was a great deal of insistence on the potential of Christianity to change history. For example, Father Carlos Alberto would emphasize the notion of the reign of God. The reign of God, he would explain, is not only the new life we are headed for. The reign of God has already begun, here on earth, and is being built right now, by the grace of God and the efforts of people. But to build the reign of God, you have to have a minimal amount of the goods of this earth, enough to be able to live with a minimum of human dignity: you had to have sanitation, health services, and schools. You had to band together in organizations, especially with the humiliated and the wronged. The reign of God was more than this, Father Carlos Alberto explained, because it included life with God, the forgiveness of sin, and a happy future for all the just. But it would not be the reign of God if it did not call for the transformation of this world as well. The demands of the reign of God generate conflict. But this is a necessary condition for genuine conversion and liberation. Jesus himself stirred up conflict. His death was not a matter of blind fate. It was the result of the intrigues of his adversaries, who felt themselves threatened by his words and deeds. And Jesus bravely accepted his suffering and death, for he was loyal to God, and he loved his sisters and brothers.

Thanks to the gospel, the little community was gradually liberated from a religion of fatalism and despondency. Now its members understood that God did not will some persons to be rich and others poor. Nor did poverty come about by spontaneous generation. Behind the poverty all around them was a great problem of injustice, along with failures in solidarity and communion. Poverty, they now saw, sprang from the unbridled greed of a few individuals. Poverty was a sin—not only an individual sin, but a group sin, in fact it was an international sin. And these humble persons, through reading and meditating on the gospel, acquired a critical awareness. They began to question land-ownership. If God has given the earth to everyone, then why do just a few persons possess nearly all of it? Why do we plant and reap, and then the landowner gets practically the whole thing? And what must we do to become more brotherly, and sisterly, to one another? What must we do to make it less difficult to love?

Father Carlos Alberto's strenuous, solitary efforts injured his health. The sacrifices he made brought him to a state of near collapse. But he succeeded in his project. Within three or four years he had guided his parishioners onto the path of liberation. There would be no turning back, ever. Suffering had dogged their steps. Every sort of obstacle had arisen. But the suffering had made sense, it had had meaning. It was a suffering that built the reign of God. Suffering is a precondition for all genuine growth. Before Father Carlos Alberto had set to work, his parishioners had been suffering meaninglessly, and they were crushed by a terrible despondency. "It is the will of God," they had said. "God assigns each of us our lot. Some are rich, some are poor." No longer.

Now there came another kind of suffering, both for the people and for Father Carlos Alberto. It was the suffering that comes of the effort to preserve the gains that one has made. It was the pain of moving ahead, the suffering that comes of defending oneself against the threatened ones who hold the power of life and death. The landlord thought of himself as a good and generous person. Not only had he given every family its own little hut, but he allowed them to plant a little piece of his land to raise food that they would actually eat themselves. Now he felt threatened. The people were toying with novelty, he said. They were going to Father's school, joining farm workers' unions, and talking about their "rights." They were becoming subversive. They were turning communist. And he promptly began to drive the workers out, burn their plots of ground, and fight the instigator of it all, Father Carlos Alberto.

The time of passion had come for all. I shall concentrate on Father Carlos, because the entire *passio populi nostri* would take the story too long. First, Father saw his community divided. The large landholders and their hangers-on no longer attended church. They began to slander the priest, accusing him first of involvement in politics, and then of subversion, in his work for justice and human rights. He had to be removed from the parish. His enemies had gone to the bishop and accused him of everything imaginable.

But the people stood behind their priest. Tensions grew. Some of the people were arrested—precisely the leaders of the gospel groups—on the pretext that they were homesteading. Some were tortured. Families were threatened. But the people stood firm. The bishop had felt obliged to transfer the priest in order to maintain order. The press mounted a campaign of vilification: the priest was using Marxist methods, the priest was a subversive. Finally Father Carlos was arrested by the security police and interrogated. He was tortured for days on end. He received visits in prison from his bishop and many of his fellow priests. On the personal level, solidarity was heartening. Few had realized how helpless they were against a power structure that forced itself on everyone, indeed that actually appealed to the sacred authority of the bishop for the legitimation and maintenance of "order"—that is, of orderly disorder.

Father Carlos Alberto was eventually released. He was assigned to another parish. And he started all over again—with the same enthusiasm, but with greater maturity and with a great deal more determination. And with a joy not of this world, for there is a joy that the world cannot give—the joy of suffering for the people's cause, of sharing in the passion of the Lord, and of having hammered out one more link in the chain of historical liberation being forged by God through the intermediary of human effort, for the subversion of every unjust order that stands in the way of the reign of God.

Father Carlos Alberto is but one priest among many in underdeveloped Latin America who continue to sacrifice themselves in this way. Nearly every Latin American country has such priests, though many have been killed. For example, Franciscan Father Ivan Bettencourt died in Central America in 1976. He had launched a project of solidarity among peasants who had been driven from their land by powerful landholders. He was seized and interrogated, to force him to confess that he was a "Marxist subversive." They cut off his ears and interrogated him. They cut off his nose and interrogated him some more. They castrated him and interrogated him some more. They cut out his tongue and declared the interrogation at an end. They sliced his body to ribbons. He was still twitching so they machine-gunned him. Finally they threw him into a well and hid the well under earth and rubble. Father Ivan died defending his brothers and sisters.

We could think we were hearing a page from the *Acts of the Martyrs* of the early days of the church, or perhaps a passage from the Letter to the Hebrews:

> Others were tortured and would not receive deliverance. . . . Still others endured mockery, scourging, even chains and imprisonment. They were stoned, sawed in two, put to death at sword's point; they went about garbed in the skins of sheep or goats, needy, afflicted, tormented. The world was not worthy of them. They wandered about in deserts and on mountains, they dwelt in caves and in holes of the earth [Heb. 11:35–38].

These are reminiscences of our glorious past of suffering and martyrdom. These are also the "acts" of the modern, anonymous saints of the church, a church being born of our longing for a greater humaneness and humanity, our desires for a truer Christianity in our countries.

A reading of the history of the Latin American church from the viewpoint of the humiliated and the wronged reveals the fuller dimensions of suffering and martyrdom in that church. It is not generally realized how many have already given their lives in the defense of the sacred rights of others—the Amerindians, the blacks, the exploited. In Rio de Janeiro from 1576 to 1680, of the eleven prelates in charge of the church there, three were forced to resign, three may have been poisoned, one had to cease his activity, and one was recalled.

The history of the Jesuits in Rio de Janeiro was no less agonizing. Several times they were threatened with expulsion from the city, and in 1640 and 1661 the threats were carried out. In 1640 they were expelled from Santos and São Paulo as well, for having tried to publicize a papal bull that had come out on the side of the Amerindians. All of these persecutions were occasioned by their struggle in defense of the Indians, the victims of the conquests that built the great Territory of Brazil on the blood of its natives.

The renowned explorer Raposo Tavares alone was responsible for the murder of fifteen thousand Amerindians and the enslavement of ten thousand more.

For defending the thesis, "No slave in Africa or Brazil is held justly," Father Gonzalo Leite (1546–1603) was punished and sent back to Portugal.

Father Antônio Vieira (1608–1697), the greatest preacher and theologian of the Brazilian colony, was so devoted to the cause of the Amerindians that he was not only persecuted, but almost lynched (for particulars, see Hoornaert).

But the great prophet of Latin America, who suffered so much persecution, who made a dozen voyages from Latin America back to Spain to plead the Amerindians' cause, was Fray Bartolomé de Las Casas (1474–1566). Among Las Casas's most authentic successors today is Dom Hélder Câmara, the greatest prophet of the Third World. He spends his life circling the globe, demonstrating the causal nexus between the opulence of the developed countries and the exploitation of the impoverished peoples of the world. The existence of rich and poor nations poses a problem of international justice, Dom Hélder explains, and points out to Christian faith the persistence of a structural sin that offends God and crushes our sisters and brothers. Dom Hélder's statements provoke all manner of persecution, detraction, death threats, pressure on groups not to let him speak, and the elimination of his very name from the media.

This kind of suffering has meaning. Death for a commitment like this is worthy. This is how all the prophets died, including the greatest of them, Jesus of Nazareth. And they will always have to suffer and die, because a system closed in upon itself and doing its best to subject history to a blind fatality will never be able to accept prophets who proclaim and seek to realize a future society with more room for God and a closer communion of brothers and sisters. This suffering is true, for it is born of the struggle with suffering. This suffering has a meaning. It is the occasion of joy and serenity. It overcomes the material factors that spawn permanent suffering, pain, and death.

No one suffers for the sake of suffering. Suffering cannot be sought for itself. Even a masochist suffers not for the sake of suffering, but for the pleasure that comes with the suffering, the pleasure that the suffering seems to generate. Suffering worthy of human beings, suffering that enhances them, rendering them like unto the suffering servant, the man of sorrows (Isa. 53:3), is the suffering that comes from a commitment to the arduous, victorious struggle with the suffering caused by the bad will of human beings who close their ears and their hearts to the prophets, persecuting them, slandering them, imprisoning them, torturing them, eliminating them. This suffering is not a matter of fate. The prophet accepts it as part of the project of liberation. It is the fruit of courageous freedom, then. It is an adult decision. This suffering nourishes human beings, making them stronger than all historical cynicism or spirit of resignation.

WHAT MAKES SUFFERING WORTHY?

What is the structure of this suffering? What is it that makes suffering worthy of a human being?

Suffering is worthy of the human being when it is for the sake of a just cause. A cause is just when it seeks justice for the exploited, when it pursues the rights of the exploited against the legality of a distorted civil order, against the tenacity of an imposed system. An oppressive system will always try to make itself look like a meaningful totality, as the truth for this historical moment, as escape and deliverance from the problems of the people. But such a system tramples human dignity under foot, reduces human beings to things, exiles them as nonpersons. A prophet like Father Carlos Alberto questions the whole of a system that refuses to open itself to human beings. His kind of questioning is part and parcel of the attitude of faith. Except for its historical content, comprising the life and lot of Jesus Christ and the people of whom he was born, Christian faith is fundamentally an attitude of breach with all closed systems.

To believe in God is to believe that something new can burst in at any moment, scattering tidy arrangements to the winds. Something new for the salvation of human life can happen at any time. And so when a system closes in upon itself, domesticates religious values, tames them, forcing God through the grid of its own realizations, then that system becomes oppressive. And then prophets rise up in the name of the sacred right of outraged humanity. Any human being's cause is God's cause. The prophets begin their denunciation, and inaugurate a new, subversive praxis. Then the prophets have to pay for the "disorder" they have caused within the "order" they have denounced as wicked.

The prophets look at the poor, encounter God there, look at society, and can then pass judgment on the whole of that society. Should they not engage in their denunciation and liberative praxis, they would feel that they had been unfaithful to God and their sisters and brothers. There is no turning back. God grasps them, and endows them with the strength, the courage, the heroism to bear up under every hardship, even death itself, with serenity and interior joy. There are values for which one must be prepared to sacrifice one's life. The glory of a violent death is worth more than the ease of an accursed liberty, as Bishop Phileas declared in his encomium on the joys of Christian martyrdom (Eusebius of Caesarea, *Ecclesiastical History*, book 8, chap. 10, nos. 9–10). The martyr for the cause of freedom is the faithful witness of that sacrosanct liberty that no one may violate or manipulate with impunity. The martyr for the cause of freedom freely and spontaneously decides to die, accepting death as a sacrament of protest against all violence. The memories left behind by martyrs are subversive. They give oppressors a bad conscience.

With prophets, with martyrs, Christian faith in the sacred Absolute that dwells both in human beings, and in a God committed to the destiny of each and every individual human being, becomes a spirituality capable of bestowing a transcendent meaning on every sorrow, every sacrifice.

Father Carlos Alberto wrote to his parents from prison:

> During the long periods of questioning to which I was subjected, my one
> determination was to state my faith convictions very clearly to a world in
> which something had gone wrong. I had no worries about how these
> convictions might be misinterpreted. I simply kept before my mind the
> testimony Christ rendered when *he* was a prisoner under sentence.
> "Blessed are you when they persecute you and revile you and speak all
> manner of evil against you for my name's sake," Christ promised. And
> he told his own disciples, "The hour will come in which those who kill
> you will think they have done something for God." It would be naive of
> me to think I'd made a Christian commitment if I excluded the way of the
> cross. Today I'm convinced that that way, however it might destroy you,
> is actually more worthwhile than any other. What really destroys you is
> trying to go another road, even if the other road offers more security.

Father Carlos Alberto was barbarously tortured and taken back to his cell.
With what strength he had left he read the passion of our Lord Jesus Christ
according to Saint John, and realized that he was identified with Christ in a
glorious suffering.

As if his first letter had been anything but clear, he wrote another: "At times
I wonder, 'How long, O Lord?' . . . And I have the distinct impression that he
has not yet required of me all I have to give." We could think we were hearing
the testimonials that fill the *Acta Martyrum*, as when the plebeian Maximus
was tortured by the Proconsul Optimus, and he taunted his torturer: "These
are not torments you pour upon me for my confession of our Lord Jesus
Christ. This is balm!" (*Lateinische Märtyrerakten*, 41).

Praxis of faith, then, rejects rigid systemization. It lives in another dimension. It lives in the reality of a new world of brotherly and sisterly communion,
a world of the reign of God over everyone who is willing to be converted to it. It
relativizes every pretension to absolute value on the part of this world. That is
why the sufferer in faith, though victimized by the violence of the system, is a
free, jovial spirit, someone grasped by the true Absolute who confers meaning
on persecution and death. The world promised by God, the world that "eye has
not seen, ear has not heard" (1 Cor. 2:9), is so real, so true, so fulfilling, that no
death, however violent, no torture, however inhuman, is experienced as destructive suffering. This free, liberating attitude exasperates the agents of the
system. It stupefies them, strikes them with wonder and incomprehension, as
we read in the account of the sufferings of Saint Polycarp (Eusebius, *Ecclesiastical History*, book 4, chap. 15, nos. 18–25). Is this not the way the Transcendent is made manifest—by shattering what everyone takes for granted? Is this
not a parousia of God as the true Lord of life and death? Police spies and
repressive forces cannot repress, cannot destroy, this dimension of gladness
and meaning. This divine parousia is their downfall. It destroys their morale.

There is another dimension of faith as lived by the free sufferer besides the dimension of faith as liberative praxis of a meaning that annihilates suffering. It is the dimension of hope. Hope transfigures the meaning of the sufferer's torments. "What is hope?" asks Rubem Alves. And he replies:

Hope is the presentiment that the imagination is more real, and reality less real, than we had thought. It is the sensation that the last word does not belong to the brutality of facts with their oppression and repression. It is the suspicion that reality is far more complex than realism would have us believe, that the frontiers of the possible are not determined by the limits of the present, and that, miraculously and surprisingly, life is readying the creative event that will open the way to freedom and resurrection [*O filho do amanhã*].

The prophet hopes. The prophet refuses to accept that this is the best of all possible worlds. The true human being has not yet been born, and we must be the midwives of that gestation and birth in history. Human beings must accomplish what not yet is but can and must be—God's historical project for them. They were created to be brothers and sisters, daughters and sons of God, and rulers of the universe in service. Christian hope appears as a prophecy about a human being who will plunge headlong toward the fulfillment of a future that is already being prepared and anticipated in the present. In the name of that hope, Father Carlos Alberto protested, denounced, and cooperated with God in the construction of a more human social enterprise. He "de-fatalized" a system that presents itself as the only choice. He liberated the future from the shackles of the ideological "necessities" and political imperatives that hold men and women in their vicelike grip. The struggle to deliver history from its dead past and oppressive present, in the name of all nonpersons, has a prophetic meaning. It keeps hope alive—that hope without which human persons would no longer see any reason to be.

Roger Garaudy, reflecting on his struggles in France and Algeria, remarked:

Once this simple truth is perceived, it changes one's whole life. Of all the miseries one has suffered, none is decisive. Everything can be overcome—crises, servitude, war itself—once one sees that all this can be contested. The Resistance, if not the proof of this, was its hope [Garaudy, *Palavra*, 182].

Further, Christian faith in salvation and liberation is based on a fundamental conviction that nothing in the world is simply fated to be. There is nothing in the universe that simply cannot be helped. No evil is so impregnable as to be absolutely irremediable. Everything is capable of renewal, and the world is destined to realize the utopia of the reign of God. The dimensions of Christian faith are not limited to the salvation history of the world of the past. Christian faith is principally centered on what is yet to come, on what must come, on what men and women must will to come. The reign of God will not come by magic. It will come as a result of the human effort that helps gestate the definitive future.

Integral salvation is not posthistorical. It is realized in a liberation process that involves moments of conflict. All historical liberation, even the liberation brought to us by Jesus Christ, occurs in the context of a covenant of suffering, pain, and death between human beings and God. Suffering is the price we have to pay for the resistance the fatalizing systems put up to each and every quantum leap in history. God spares no one this suffering, this sacrifice—not even his well-beloved Son. But this is not "harmless," meaningless suffering. It is pregnant with meaning. It is part of a liberation project. It is an expression of loyalty and fidelity to the cause of justice and truth.

The attitude of the just in apparent defeat has an efficiency all its own, different from the efficiency of violence in modifying situations and eliminating opponents. The effectiveness of violence is illusory. It fails to stop the spiral of violence. The effectiveness of suffering in consequence of having worked for a just cause is less visible, but it is genuine. It demonstrates that what is in store for human beings, what is desirable for human beings, is on the side of right, justice, love, and communion, and not on the side of greed, violence, and the will to power. No wonder, then, that closed systems grow more and more violent as they approach their inevitable end.

MYSTERY OF THE PASSION OF THE WORLD

In light of the experience of a suffering that dignifies, it will be in place to come down to certain more radical questions. What is the ultimate meaning of the *passio mundi*? Is there really nothing for it but resignation and cynicism? The suffering just ask—and their question adds to their suffering: Why have human beings such an astonishing capacity for resistance to truth? Why do they become so blind, aggressive, vicious, and destructive? It is estimated that known wars have eliminated more than three and a half billion persons. Can we have the heart to speak of "peace" and "liberation"? Of the more than three and a half billion persons who presently populate the earth, some one billion of them suffer from extreme poverty, and about eight hundred million are illiterate. Can we identify the particular individuals who are responsible for such structures of violence? Can we find the oppressors?

A careful reading of reality convinces me that the problem does not lie with individuals. What good will it do to eliminate the individual oppressor when the oppressive structure of which the individual is but an agent continues to guarantee oppression? We labor under an illusion if we hope to join battle against the evil of the world with a blind, vengeful assault on individuals. We must have some historical perspective. These persons are not the producers of the drama; they are but players on the stage. The more profound drama is social reality itself. It is the very structure of the system that is wicked. Only by coming down to an analysis of the system, and launching a different, alternative praxis, shall we be able to combat evils meaningfully and effectively.

At the same time, the structural answer is inadequate to explain the colossal human resistance to a qualitative transformation of society in terms of humanity and justice. Social structure has a history that has been centuries in the weaving. It is the fruit of a historical project, and has deep, mysterious ties to human freedom. Here the problem becomes extremely difficult. Where is the responsibility to be lodged? Surely there is a personal, individual dimension in this responsibility. No one is a robot. We all accept, assimilate, reject, and accommodate to things, in function of our own personal project. Of course, there is a structural, collective dimension as well, a responsibility handed down from the past, impregnating the heart of current structures and penetrating the heart of every individual. How can the history of freedom have taken such a painful route? How can it have generated the system of evil of our everyday experience? As the Second Vatican Council says, the human being "is incapable of battling the assaults of evil successfully, so that everyone feels as though . . . bound by chains" (*Gaudium et Spes*, no. 13).

Here we are dealing with the essential, radical problem of the conditions for the possibility of evil and sin. Perhaps we ought to see this possibility in the mere fact of creaturely being. Ontologically, the essence of creatureliness is corruptibility. Scholasticism saw this very well, and posited a metaphysical evil independent of human spontaneity, one that preexists the creation of the human being, an evil not committed by human liberty but simply part and parcel of the ontological state of the mystery we call creation. Simply by the fact of not being God, the universe is limited and dependent, separated from God, distinct from God, different from God. However perfect it may be, the universe is never the perfection of God. Before God it is always imperfect. This evil is the *conscious* finitude of the world, which constitutes the limitation experienced as suffering by conscious life. As Hegel observed: "All consciousness of life is consciousness of the evil of life."

Consciousness is finite. But it can experience itself as finite only against the background of an experience of the Infinite. This disparity between our experiences of the finite and the Infinite provokes suffering. This is "ontological pain." This suffering, however, belongs to human dignity. This suffering is an expression of our humanness. As the experience of the fleetingness of the world of persons and of love, it is our invitation to open ourselves to the Absolute. This suffering anticipates death as an opportunity to be totally within the Infinite, totally in God.

From this viewpoint death is a good—part and parcel of our mortal life, and constitutes the opportunity for our maximal "hominization," in God. Just so, far from being a foretaste of the destructive action of death, suffering can actually render our self-liberation more intense, bestowing on us a freedom for the Freedom that is God. All suffering can have this structure, even the anonymous, anything but heroic, silent, everyday suffering of our limited existence. Suffering and ontological evil become the seedbed of hope. They free the imagination, and we dream dreams of total liberation. They point to the human being's creational captivity, and this shows the way, in hope and desire, to complete liberation.

This innocent evil causes us no problems. This evil merely constitutes the necessary condition for evil as sin, evil as the fruit of the abuse of human freedom. The created creators called human beings can refuse to accept the evil and suffering arising from their ontological, creaturely condition. They can reject their finitude and their mortality. They can wish to be as God (Gen. 3:5). As God? How is that? God is precisely what human beings cannot be—infinite, immortal, uncaused cause. Sin consists in seeking the impossible, seeking to be what God is. Sin is the basic refusal to accept the human condition, with its limitations and its consciousness of its limitations (the source of ontological suffering and pain). Sin is the attempt, absurd because impossible, to effectuate oneself—to be what human beings can never be: their own fundament, absolutely *in-dependent* (literally, "not hanging" from anything): their own creators.

All sin is an aberration, a wandering away, from the meaning of creation—a violent separation from God and selfish return to, turning in upon, oneself. This project has its own history. The warp and woof of what it is to be human is shot through with this "sin of the world." This is original sin—the antihistory of the absurd, the history of the irrational force that oppresses human beings. This is the evil that generates suffering as the fruit of selfishness, the upshot of the will to power and domination. This evil is captivity without dignity, a senseless suffering, a useless pain. Original sin generates suffering as destruction of life, as oppression in the form of domination over the freedom of others, as a morbid structure pervading history and holding a dismaying proportion of humanity in its shackles.

With this reflection, we collide with the mystery of human freedom. We have a sensation of impotence. Are the destinies of history handed over to the caprice of the mighty?

No, we reply, this is a historical phenomenon. It can be combated, then, forced back within its historical limits. True, we cannot ignore its prevalence in history. Be our commitment ever so intense, then, we may not allow our enthusiasm to send us galloping off after utopias, as if it were within our power totally to eradicate the evil of the world. But we must have courage for the provisional. We must have the determination to take concrete steps to overcome situations of enslavement, and then we must have heroic patience to bear up under the torturing presence of the persistence of evil, refusing to let it contaminate our hope and our will to fight. This is the meaning of the Christian message as germ of hope. The Lord is risen. He has demonstrated his power over the dismal dimension of sin and death that springs from human hate. Jesus' Johannine statement is more than mere phraseology: it is the ratification of an experience of Easter. "You will suffer in the world. But take courage! I have overcome the world" (John 16:33).

Only in a battle against evil, only in feeling its resistance, does a radical reflection on the *passio mundi* become legitimate. Divorced from this battle our reflection would become ideology, and enervate our strength for the combat. This *passio mundi* is not a problem, but a mystery, inaccessible to discursive, analytical reason—a mystery as deep as the mystery of a human freedom that manifests itself now as love and now as hate.

I began this chapter with a story. It seemed to me that a symbolic event taken from real life would be more suggestive of an adequate view of the mystery of suffering than pure speculation would be. As Paul Ricoeur said, symbols and myths "make you think." Thinking radically always means thinking mystery, thinking within mystery, thinking in order to gain access to the depths of mystery. Thinking radically has nothing to do with eliminating mystery. Faced with the mystery of the pain and suffering of millions, and of the difficulties in the struggle, we can only beseech God: From these frightening billows draw us not; only deliver us from the fear that would drown us.

Chapter 10

How to Preach the Cross of Jesus Christ Today

As I come to the end of this study on the relationship between the passion of Christ and the passion of the world, I want to draw some conclusions with respect to preaching the cross in the world of today—in this world that cries for deliverance from the cross.

First of all, as we have seen, we must enlarge our concept of the cross and of death. *Death* is more than the last moment of life. We die all our lives. Life begins to be limited the moment it is born, and continues acquiring limitations until it finally succumbs to the last, the final limit. To ask how Christ died, then, is tantamount to asking how he lived—how he took up the conflicts of life, how he embraced the journey of life that comes to an end only when one's dying is complete. And the answer is: Christ embraced death just as he embraced whatever life brought him: his joys and his sorrows, his conflicts and his confrontations for the sake of his message and his life, his way of living.

It is somewhat the same with the cross. The cross is more than a piece of wood. It is the embodiment of human hatred, violence, and criminality. The cross is anything that limits life (we speak of "life's crosses"), everything that makes us suffer, everything that makes the journey hard because of ill will on the part of human beings (we know that we are to "take up our cross daily").

How did Christ carry the cross, then? He did not seek the cross for its own sake. On the contrary, his goal was a spirit that would avoid manufacturing crosses for himself and others. He prayed and lived love. One who loves, one who serves, does not create crosses for others. One who loves and serves does not generate a poor quality of life for others. No, Christ proclaimed the gospel, the good news, of the Life and Love that are God. To these he committed himself. But the world closed itself to him. The world created crosses for him along his road, and finally lifted him up on the wood of the cross itself. The cross was the outcome of a proclamation that asked questions. The cross was the consequence of a practice of liberation. When that cross came, Christ refused to flee, refused to temporize, refused to abandon his proclamation and

129

his witness, crucify him though it might. He continued to love, in spite of the hatred that was overwhelming him. He took up his cross in token of fidelity to God and human beings. He was crucified for God in the sense of being faithful to God. He was crucified by and for human beings in the sense of loving them and being faithful to them.

To preach the cross of our Lord Jesus Christ today entails the following:

1) To commit oneself and all one's energies for a world where love, peace, and a community of sisters and brothers, a world where openness and self-surrender to God, will be less difficult. This means denouncing situations that generate hatred, division, and practical atheism—atheism in terms of structures, values, practices, and ideologies. It means proclaiming, and practicing— in commitment, love, and solidarity—justice in the family, in the school, in the economic system, and in political relations. The consequence of this engagement will be crisis, suffering, confrontation, and the cross. Acceptance of the cross of this clash, this confrontation, is what it means to carry the cross as our Lord carried it: it means suffering, enduring, for the sake of the cause we support and the life we lead.

2) The suffering that comes with this commitment, the cross to be carried down this road, is suffering and martyrdom for God and God's cause in the world. These martyrs are martyrs for God. They are not martyrs for the system. They are martyrs *of* the system, but *for* God. Those who suffer and are crucified for the sake of the justice of this world, then, are God's witnesses. They break open the closed system that holds itself out as just, fraternal, and good. Those who suffer and are martyred for justice, after the fashion of Jesus and of all who follow him, dis-cover the future—leave history open, so that it can grow and produce more justice than at present, more love than prevails in society as yet. The system seeks to close the future. It tries to "put a lid" on it. The system is fatalistic: it judges that there is no need of freedom and modification. One who bears the cross and suffering of the struggle with this intrasystemic fatalism carries the cross and suffers with Jesus and as Jesus. To suffer thus is honorable. To die thus is a death worth dying.

3) To carry the cross as Jesus carried it, then, means taking up a solidarity with the crucified of this world—with those who suffer violence, who are impoverished, who are dehumanized, who are offended in their rights. To carry the cross as Jesus carried it means to defend these persons, and to attack the practices in whose name they are made nonpersons. It means taking up the cause of their liberation, and suffering for the sake of this cause. This is what it means to carry the cross. Jesus' cross and death, too, were the consequence of such a commitment to the deserted of this world.

4) To suffer thus, to die for the sake of other crucified persons, involves bearing the heavy burden of the system's inversion of values, the cross of the warped hierarchy of values against which one has committed oneself. The system calls those who take up the cause of the lowly and the defenseless "subversives, traitors, enemies of the human race, damned by religion and abandoned by God." ("Cursed be he who hangs on the tree!") Horrors! These

persons want to revolutionize the established order! But the reason why the sufferer, the martyr, opposes the system and denounces its values and practices is because it constitutes an ordering precisely of disorder. What the system labels "just, fraternal, and good" is in reality unjust, arbitrary, and evil. The martyr rips the mask from the face of the system. Martyrs suffer for the sake of a greater justice, for the sake of another order ("If your justice abound not more than that of the Pharisees . . ."). These are those who suffer without hating, who bear the cross without fleeing: for they bear it out of love for the truth and love for the crucified persons for whom they have risked their personal security and their very life. This is what Jesus does, and this is what every follower of his must do, all down through history. They suffer as the damned; actually they are the blessed. They die as if abandoned; in reality it is they who are the accepted of God. Thus does God confound the wisdom and justice of this world.

5) The cross, then, is the symbol of the rejection and violation of the sacred rights of God and the human being. It is the product of hatred. There are those who, committing themselves to the struggle to abolish the cross of the world, themselves have to suffer and bear the cross. The cross is imposed upon them, inflicted on them, by the creators of crosses. But this cross is accepted. Not because a value is seen in it, but because there are those who burst asunder the logic of its violence by their love. To accept the cross is to be greater than the cross. To live thus is to be stronger than death.

6) To preach the cross can mean to be invited to perform the extreme act of love and trust, in a total de-centering of self. Life has its traumatic side. There are those who are vanquished in their battle for a just cause, who are deprived of all hope, who are in prison for life, or who have been sentenced to a sure death. Indeed, all of those who struggle for the cause of justice must either carry the cross onerously, or hang upon it helplessly. How often we must assist at this human drama silent and impotent! Anything we might say by way of an attempt to console will seem empty chatter. Any deed of solidarity will seem ineffective resignation. Thought strangles word. Perplexity stifles tears at their source. There is a pain and a death at the hands of injustice that shreds the heart: the conclusion of the drama is foregone, and there is no escape.

Even so, the drama has a meaning. All cynicism, resignation, and despair notwithstanding, it remains meaningful to speak of the cross. The drama is not necessarily a tragedy. Jesus Christ passed through all this. He transfigured suffering, pain, and condemnation to death by transforming them into acts of freedom and a love of self-surrender—by transforming them into a way to God and a new approach to those who rejected him. He forgave the rejecters, and abandoned himself in trust and confidence to One who is greater.

Forgiveness is love in pain. A trusting self-abandon is the total de-centration of ourselves and our total recentering on Someone who infinitely transcends us. Forgiveness and self-surrender mean risking Mystery, throwing in our lot with that ultimate vessel of Meaning in which we participate more than we dream. This is the opportunity offered to human freedom. Men and women can take advantage of the offer, and rest secure. Or they can let it slip by, and founder in despair. Forgiveness and trust are our tools for not letting hopelessness have the last word. They constitute the supreme deed of human grandeur.

How do we know that this trust, this de-centering, achieves ultimate Meaning? By the resurrection. Resurrection is the fullness and manifestation of the Life that resonates within life and within death. The only way for the Christian to make this assertion is to look at the crucified Jesus—who now lives.

7) To die thus is to live. Within this death on a cross is a life that cannot be stamped out, a life that lies hidden in death itself. This life does not come after death. This life is found in the life of love, solidarity, and courage that has so suffered and so died. This is the life that, in death, is revealed in its power and its glory.

This is what Saint John means when he tells us that Jesus' being lifted up on the cross is glorification, and that this "hour" is at once the time of passion and of transfiguration. A unity, then, a oneness prevails between passion and resurrection, life and death. To live and be crucified for the sake of justice and for God's sake is to live. This is why the message of the passion is always accompanied by the message of the resurrection. Those who have died in rebellion against the system of this world, those who have refused to enter into and connive with this world, who have refused to fit into the schemata of this world (Rom. 12:2), are the risen ones. Insurrection for the cause of God and neighbor is resurrection. Death may look meaningless. Yet it is death that has a future, for it is death that guards and protects the meaning of history.

8) To preach the cross, today, is to preach the following of Jesus. This is not "dolorism," this is not the exaltation of the negative. This is the proclamation of positivity, of a commitment to make it gradually impossible for human beings to crucify other human beings. But this struggle involves the cross. It means carrying that cross with courage, and hanging upon it with constancy. Thus to live is resurrection achieved. Thus to live is to live a life founded in the Life that no cross can crucify, but can only reveal as still more victorious. To preach the cross, then, means this, and this alone: to follow Jesus. And to follow Jesus is to take *(per-seguir)* his path, pursue *(pro-seguir)* his cause, and achieve *(con-seguir)* his victory.

9) God is not indifferent to the pain of the victims of history. Out of love and solidarity (cf. John 3:16), God becomes poor, is condemned, crucified, and murdered. God has taken on a reality that objectively contradicts God. Why does God do so? Because God does not wish some human beings to impoverish and crucify other human beings. Thus are we shown that God's preferred mediation is neither the glory of history nor the transparency of historical meaning. God's preferred mediation is the concrete, real-life suffering of the oppressed. "If God has loved us so, we must have the same love for one another" (1 John 4:11). To draw near to God is to draw near the oppressed (Matt. 25), and vice versa. To say that God took up the cross must not be a glorification or eternalization of the cross. That God has taken up

the cross shows only how much God loves. God loves sufferers so much that he suffers and dies along with them.

But neither, on the other hand, is God indifferent to crime—to the negative weight in the balance of history. God does not allow the wound to fester until the manifestation of justice at the end of the world. God intervenes and justifies, in the risen Jesus, all the impoverished and crucified of history. The meaning of the resurrection is that justice and love, and the struggles waged for both, have meaning. Their future is guaranteed. Justice, love, and our struggles to attain them only appear to have failed in the process of history. They shall triumph. Good, and good alone, shall reign.

Chapter 11

Conclusion – the Cross: Mystery and Mysticism

To live the cross of our Lord Jesus Christ involves a mysticism of life. This mysticism rests on a mystery—of a life generated where death appears, of love amid hatred. The cross is all this. The cross is mystery and mysticism.

On the one side, the cross is a symbol of the mystery of a human freedom in rebellion. The cross emerges from a will to rejection, a will to vengeance, to self-assertion to the point of eliminating the other. The cross is what human beings can do when they refuse themselves to God. Therefore the cross is the symbol of the fallen human being, inhuman-being. The cross is the symbol of crime.

On the other side, the cross is the symbol of the mystery of human freedom in its power. When borne by a commitment to overcome it, to make it gradually less viable in the world, the cross is the symbol of a new kind of life, a life centered outside oneself, the life of the prophet, the martyr, the man or woman of the kingdom of God. This is the life that, although doing nothing to provoke the cross, bears it—but in bearing it combats it, and in combating it becomes its victim, crucified by the fury of those who have hardened their heart to their brother and sister and God. But crucified, this life can transfigure its cross, and make it a sacrifice of love for others. Thus the cross is the symbol of the human being new and alive. The cross is the symbol of love.

Each cross, then, contains a denunciation and a call. It denounces a human closing-in upon oneself to the point of crucifying God. It appeals for a love that can bear all things, a love of the kind with which the Father delivered his own Son to death for the sake of his enemies. And so the cross is essentially ambiguous, and the maintenance of this ambiguity is the condition for the preservation of its critical character, its function as the refining fire both of the pretensions of human self-assertion, and of our image of an impassible God, a God untouched by the suffering of the crucified of history. God can suffer.

And so, we see, every cross has two sides. On the back, naked and solitary, the cross looks out upon human hatred. On the front, someone lives and suffers, facing love, human and divine.

The paradox of the cross is incomprehensible both to formal and to dialectical reason. It is beyond the abstract *logos*. The cross has its own *logos*, the *logos tou staurou*, the logic (word) of the cross (1 Cor. 1:18). Here is a logic assimilable only through praxis: by combating and taking up, accepting, the cross and death. Just as no starveling's hunger is appeased by discourses upon the culinary art, so neither is the problem of suffering resolved by reflection upon it. It is by eating that hunger is alleviated. It is by struggling that evil and its character of absurdity are overcome.

Paul lived what he preached:

> We are afflicted in every way possible, but we are not crushed; full of doubts, we never despair. We are persecuted but never abandoned; we are struck down but never destroyed. . . . Dead, yet here we are, alive; punished, but not put to death; sorrowful, though we are always rejoicing; poor, yet we enrich many. We seem to have nothing, yet everything is ours! [2 Cor. 4:8–9, 6:9–10].

This is the praxis that reveals what is concealed in the drama of the cross and death: ultimate Meaning and Life.

Nudus nudo sequi—naked in the following of the naked One. Behold the mysticism and the mystery of the cross.

Bibliographic References

Audet, Jean Paul. *The Gospel Project*. New York: Paulist, 1969.

Aulen, Gustaf. *Christus Victor: An Historical Study of the Three Main Types of Atonement*. New York: Macmillan, 1974.

Belo, Fernando. *A Materialist Reading of the Gospel of Mark*. Maryknoll, N.Y.: Orbis, 1981.

Benoit, Pierre. *Paixão e ressurreição do Senhor*. São Paulo, 1975.

———. "Le Procès de Jésus," in *Exégèse et Théologie*, 1:265–89. Paris, 1961.

———. "Zur theologischen Bedeutung des Todes Jesu," *Herderkorrespondenz*, 26 (1972) 149–54.

Berger, Klaus. *Die Gesetzauslegung Jesu*, vol. 1. Neukirchen: Neukirchener, 1972.

Best, Ernest. *The Temptation and the Passion: The Markan Soteriology*. Cambridge University Press, 1965.

Blinzler, Josef. *The Trial of Jesus: The Jewish and Roman Proceedings against Jesus Christ Described and Assessed from the Oldest Accounts*. Westminster, Md.: Newman, 1959.

Boff, Clodovis. "Foi Jesus um revolucionário?" *Revista Eclesiástica Brasiliera*, 31 (1971) 97–118. With abundant bibliographical references.

Boff, Leonardo. *Jesus Christ Liberator*, pp. 63–120. Maryknoll, N.Y.: Orbis, 1978.

———. *A ressurreição de Cristo e a nossa ressurreição na morte*. Petrópolis, Brazil: Vozes, 1972.

———. "Salvação em Jesus Cristo e processo de libertação," *Concilium* (Lisbon), 6 (1974) 753–64.

———. *Teologia do cativeiro e da libertação*. Lisbon, 1976.

———, et al. *Experimentar Deus hoje*. Petrópolis, Brazil: Vozes, 1975.

Breton, Stanislas. *Passion du Christ et les philosophies*. Edizioni "Eco." Teramo, Italy: San Gabriele del l'Addolorata, 1954.

Bultmann, Rudolf. *Die Geschichte der synoptischen Tradition*. Göttingen, 6th ed., 1964. English translation: *History of the Synoptic Tradition*. New York: Harper & Row, 1968.

Câmara, Hélder. *Revolution through Peace*. World Perspectives, 45. New York, Evanston, San Francisco, London: Harper & Row, 1971.

Chevallier, Max-Alain. *La prédication de la croix*. Paris: Cerf, 1971.

Cone, James H. *A Black Theology of Liberation*. Philadelphia and New York: Lippincott, 1970.

Conzelmann, Hans. *Zur Bedeutung des Todes Jesu*, pp. 35–54: "Historie und Theologie in den synoptischen Passionsberichten." Gütersloh: Gütersloher, 1967.

Cousin, Hugues. *Le Prophète assassiné*. Paris: Delarge, 1976.

Cullmann, Oscar. *Jesus and the Revolutionaries*. New York: Harper & Row, 1970.

137

Delling, Gerhard. *Der Kreuzestod Jesu in der urchristlichen Verkündigung.* Berlin: Vandenhoeck & Ruprecht, 1971.

Dibelius, Martin. *Botschaft und Geschichte,* vol. 1. Tübingen, 1953. English translation: *The Message of Jesus Christ: The Tradition of the Early Christian Communities.* New York: Scribner's, 1939.

———. *Die Formgeschichte des Evangeliums.* Tübingen, 1933. English translation: *From Tradition to Gospel.* Greenwood, S.C.: Attic Press, 1982.

Dodd, C.H. *According to the Scriptures: The Sub-Structure of New Testament Theology.* London: Nisbet, 1952.

Dumas, Benoit A. *Los dos rostros alienados de la Iglesia una: ensayo del teoloía política.* Buenos Aires: Latinoamerica Libros, 1971.

Dupont, Jacques. *Les Béatitudes.* Paris: Gabalda, 1969.

Duquoc, Christian. *Christologie: Essai dogmatique.* Vol. 2: *Messie.* Paris: Cerf, 1972.

———. "Cruz de Cristo e sofrimento humano," *Concilium* (Lisbon), 119 (1976) 77–85.

———. *Jesus, homem livre.* Lisbon, 1973. French version: *Jésus, homme libre: esquisse d'une christologie.* Paris: Cerf, 1978.

Ellacuría, Ignacio. *Caracter político de la misión de Jesús.* MIEC-JECI Documento 13–14. Lima: MIEC-JECI, 1974.

Fascher, Erich. *Neutestamentliche Studien zu Rudolf Bultmann,* pp. 228ff.: "Theologische Beobachtungen." Berlin, 1957.

Ferraro, B. "A significação política da morte de Jesus à luz do Novo Testamento," *Revista Eclesiástica Brasileira,* 36 (1976) 811–57.

Feuillet, André. "La coupe et le baptème de la Passion," *Revue Biblique,* 74 (1967) 365–91.

Fischer, K. "Der Tod Jesu heute: Warum musste Jesus sterben?," *Orientierung an Jesus,* 35 (1971) 196–99.

Flender, Helmut. *Die Botschaft Jesu von der Gottesherrschaft.* Munich: Kaiser, 1968.

Garaudy, Roger. *Palavra de homem.* Lisbon, 1975. French original: *Parole d'homme.* Paris: Laffont, 1975.

George, Augustin. "Comment Jésus a-t-il perçu sa propre mort?" *Lumière et vie,* 20 (1971) 34–59.

Gerhardsson, Birger. "Jesus Livré et abandonné," *Revue Biblique,* 76 (1969) 222–25.

Gese, Hartmut. "Psalm 22 und das NT," *Zeitschrift für Theologie und Kirche,* 63 (1968) 1–22.

Gils, Félix. "Le sabbat a été fait pour l'homme et non l'homme pour le sabbat," *Revue Biblique,* 69 (1962) 506–23.

Gironés, Gonzalo. *Jesucristo: Tratado de soteriología critológica.* Anales del Seminario Metropolitano. Valencia, 1973.

Gnilka, Joachim. *Jesus Christus nach frühen Zeugnissen des Glaubens,* pp. 110–27: "Das Christusbild der Spruchquelle." Munich: Kösel, 1970.

———. "Mein Gott, mein Gott," *Biblische Zeitschrift,* 3 (1959) 294–97.

Gonçalves, Oliveira Leite. *Jesus e a constestação política.* Petrópolis, Brazil: Vozes, 1974.

Goppelt, Leonhard. *Theology of the New Testament.* Grand Rapids: Eerdmans, 1982.

Greshake, Gisbert. "Der Wandel der Erlösungsvorstellungen." In Rudolph Affemann et al., *Erlösung und Emanzipation,* pp. 69–101. Freiburg: Herder, 1973.

Grillmeier, Alois. *Der Logos am Kreuz: zur christologischen Symbolik der älteren Kreuzigungsdarstellung.* Munich: Hueber, 1956.

Guénon, René. *Symbolism of the Cross.* London: Luzac, 1975.

Hedinger, Ulrich. *Wider die Versöhnung Gottes mit dem Elend: eine Kritik des christlichen Theismus und A-theismus.* Zurich: Theologischer, 1972.

Hengel, Martin. *Was Jesus a Revolutionist?* Philadelphia: Fortress, 1971.

Hofius, Otfried. *Jesu Tischgemeinschaft mit den Sündern.* Stuttgart: Calwer, 1967.

Hoornaert, E. "A tradição lascasiana no Brasil," *Revista Eclesiástica Brasileira,* 35 (1975) 379–89.

Jeremias, Joachim. *Der Opfertod Jesu Christi.* Stuttgart, 1963.

———. *Teología del Nuevo Testamento,* 1:134–38: "Quiénes son los pobres?" Salamanca, 1974. English translation: *New Testament Theology.* Vol. 1, *The Proclamation of Jesus.* New York: Scribner's, 1971.

———. "Zöllner und Sünder," *Zeitschrift für Neutestamentliche Wissenschaft,* 30 (1931) 209–300.

Kamp, J. *Souffrance de Dieu, vie du monde.* Paris: Casterman, 1971.

Kessler, Hans. *Erlösung als Befreiung.* Düsseldorf: Patmos, 1972.

———. *Die theologische Bedeutung des Todes Jesu: eine traditionsgeschichtliche Untersuchung.* Düsseldorf: Patmos, 1970.

Klappert, Berthold. *Diskussion um Kreuz und Auferstehung.* Wuppertal: Aussaat, 1967.

Knörzer, Wolfgang: *Reich Gottes: Traum, Hoffnung, Wirklichkeit.* Stuttgart, 1969.

Konings, Johan. *Jesus nos evangelhos sinóticos.* Porto Alegre, Brazil: Pontifícia Universidade Cathólica do Rio Grande do Sul, Instituto de Teologia e Ciências Religiosas, 1974.

Kuhn, Karl Georg. "Jesus in Gethsemani," *Evangelische Theologie,* 12 (1952) 260–85.

Küng, Hans. *On Being a Christian,* pp. 419–36 ("Interpretations of Death"); 570–81 ("Coping with the Negative Side": "Misused Cross," "Misunderstood Cross," "Understood Cross"). Garden City, N.Y.: Doubleday, 1968.

———. Kasper, Walter, and Moltmann, Jürgen. *Sulla teologia della croce.* Brescia, 1974.

Kuss, Otto. *Der Brief an die Hebräer.* Regensburger Neues Testament, 8. Regensburg: Pustet, 1966.

Lateinische Märtyrerakten. Munich, 1961.

Léon-Dufour, Xavier. *The Gospels and the Jesus of History,* translated and edited by John McHugh, New York: Desclée, 1967.

Lesbaupin, Ivo. *A bem-aventuraça da persequição.* Petrópolis, Brazil: Vozes, 1975. English translation: *Blessed are the Persected.* Maryknoll, N.Y.: Orbis, 1987.

Linnemann, Eta. *Studien zur Passionsgeschichte.* Göttingen: Vandenhoeck & Ruprecht, 1970.

Lohse, Eduard. *History of the Suffering and Death of Jesus Christ.* Philadelphia: Fortress, 1967.

Mahieu, L. "L'abandon du Christ sur la croix," *Mélanges de Sciences Religieuses,* 2 (1945) 209–42.

Maldonado, Luís. *La violencia de lo sagrado: crueldad "versus" oblatividad o el ritual del sacrificio.* Salamanca: Sígueme, 1974.

Metz, Johannes B. *Erlösung und Emanzipation.* Quaestiones Disputatae, 61, pp. 120–40: "Erlösung und Emanzipation." Freiburg: Herder, 1973.

———. "Futuro que brota da recordação do sofrimento," *Concilium* (Lisbon), 6 (1972) 709–24.

———. "Pequena apologia da narração," *Concilium* (Lisbon), 5 (1973) 580–92.

Miranda, José Porfirio. *Being and the Messiah.* Maryknoll, N.Y.: Orbis, 1977.

Moltmann, Jürgen. *The Crucified God: The Cross of Christ as the Foundation and Criticism of Christian Theology.* New York, Evanston, San Francisco, London: Harper & Row, 1974.

Murphy, T. Austin. *"The Dereliction of Christ on the Cross."* Washington, D.C., 1940.

Paul, André. "Pluralité des interprétations théologiques de la mort du Christ dans le Nouveau Testament," *Lumière et Vie*, 101 (1971) 18–33.

Percy, Vincent. *Die Botschaft Jesu.* Lund: Gleerup, 1953.

Pesch, Rudolf. "Das Zöllnergastmahl (Mk 2, 15-17)," *Mélanges bibliques offerts au R.P.B. Rigaux*, pp. 63–87. Gembloux, 1970.

Popkes, Wiard. *Christus Traditus: Eine Untersuchung zum Begriff der Dahingabe im Neuen Testament.* Zurich and Stuttgart: Zwingli, 1967.

Rahner, Hugo. *Greek Myths and Christian Mystery.* New York: Biblo and Tannen, 1971.

Rahner, Karl. *Schriften zur Theologie*, vol. 8, pp. 218–35 ("Der eine Mittler und die Vielfalt der Vermittlungen"). Einsiedeln, 1967.

——, and Thüsing, Wilhelm. *A New Christology.* New York: Seabury, 1980.

Renoux, Charles. "Crucifié dans la création entière," *Bulletin de Littérature Ecclésiastique*, 1976, pp. 119–22.

Richard, Louis. *The Mystery of the Redemption.* Baltimore: Helicon, 1966.

Richardson, Alan, ed. *Theological Word Book of the Bible.* New York: Macmillan, 1960.

Rivière, Jean. *Le dogme de la rédemption: étude théologique.* Paris: Lecoffre, 1931.

——. "Rédemption." In *Dictionnaire de Théologie Catholique*, 20/2:1912-57. Paris: Letouzey et Ané, 1953-72.

Romer, K.J. *Esperar contra toda esperança.* CRB 2. Rio de Janeiro, 1973.

Ruppert, Lothar. *Jesus als der leidende Gerechte? Der Weg Jesu im Lichte eines alt- und zwischentestamentlichen Motivs.* Stuttgart: KBW, 1972.

Sabiduria de la Cruz. Revista de Espiritualidad, 139 (1976).

Schelkle, Karl Hermann. *Die Passion Jesu in der Verkündigung des Neuen Testaments: Ein Beitrag zur Formgeschichte und zur Theologie des Neuen Testaments.* Heidelberg: Kerle, 1949.

Schenke, Ludger. *Der gekreuzigte Christus: Versuch einer literarkritischen und traditionsgeschichtlichen Bestimmung der vormarkinischen Passionsgeschichte.* Stuttgart: KBW, 1974.

Schille, G. "Das Leiden des Herrn: Die evangelische Passionstradition und ihr Sitz im Leben," *Zeitschrift für Theologie und Kirche*, 52 (1955) 161–202.

Schillebeeckx, Edward. *Jesus. Die Geschichte von einem Lebenden.* Freiburg, 1974. English version: *Jesus: An Experiment in Christology.* New York: Seabury, 1968.

——. "The Mystery of Injustice and the Mystery of Mercy: Questions Concerning Human Suffering," *Stauros Bulletin* (Louvain), 3 (1975).

Schrage, Wolfgang. "Das Verständnis des Todes Jesu Christi im Neuen Testament," in Ernst Bizer et al., *Das Kreuz Jesu Christi als Grund des Heiles*, pp. 49–90. Gütersloh: Gütersloher, 1967.

Schürmann, Heinz. *Jesu Ureigener Tod: Exegetische Besinnungen.* Freiburg, Basel, and Vienna: Herder, 1975.

Sobrino, Jon. *Christology at the Crossroads: A Latin American Approach*, Maryknoll, N.Y.: Orbis, 1978.

Sofrimento e fé cristã. Concilium (Lisbon), 119 (1976).

Sölle, Dorothee. *Suffering.* Philadelphia: Fortress, 1984.

Taylor, Vincent. *The Gospel according to St. Mark.* New York: Macmillan, 1966.

van Bavel, Tarsicius J. "Teologia della croce," *Bolletino Stauros* (Pescara, Italy), 1 (1975).

Vanhoye, Albert. *De Narrationibus Passionis Christi in Evangeliis Synopticis*, pp. 28–41. Rome: Pontificio Istituto Biblico, 1970.

————. "Structure et théologie des récits de la passion dans les évangiles synoptiques," *Nouvelle Revue Théologique*, 99 (1967) 135–67.

Vidales, Raul. "La prática histórica de Jesús," *Christus* (Mexico City), 40 (1975) 43–55.

Viering, Fritz Christian. *Der Kreuzestod Jesu: Interpretation eines theologischen Gutachtens.* Gütersloh: Gütersloher, 1969.

Vögtle, Anton. *Das Neue Testament und die Zukunft des Kosmos.* Düsseldorf: Patmos, 1972.

von Balthasar, Hans Urs. "Mysterium Paschale," in Johannes Feiner and Magnus Löhrer, eds., *Mysterium Salutis*, vol. 3/6. Petrópolis, Brazil: Vozes, 1974.

Wilckens, Ulrich. *Weisheit und Torheit: eine exegetisch-religionsgeschichtliche Untersuchung zu 1. Kor. 1 und 2.* Tübingen: Mohr, 1959.

Willems, Bonifac A., and Weier, R. *Soteriologie von der Reformation bis zur Gegenwart. Handbuch der Dogmengeschichte*, 3/2. Freiburg: Herder, 1972.

Zum Verständnis des Todes Jesu. Stellungnahme des Theologischen Ausschusses und Beschluss der Synode der Evangelischen Kirche der Union. Gütersloh: Gütersloher, 1968.

Scripture Index

Compiled by James Sullivan

OLD TESTAMENT